DON'T UNRAVEL
When You Travel

CIDER MILL
PRESS

BOOK
PUBLISHERS

Kennebunkport, ME

DON'T UNRAVEL
When You Travel

Joe Rhatigan & Susan A. McBride

For Margaret Rose,
the best travel companion ever.

S.A.M.

For Kayleigh, Evan & Maggie, my crazy
creative team. I love you!

J.R.

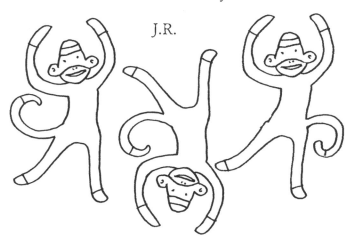

Introducing . . .

More Fun Than You Can Shake a Stick At!

There's nothing quite like going on a trip. The anticipation! The packing! Daydreaming about all the fun you'll have! The one part people often forget to plan for is the *getting there*, which can: Frazzle your nerves! Upset your stomach! Bore you to tears!

Whether you're taking a trip across town to Grandma's house or going on a cruise around the world, this book will be your best travel companion. While other kids are unraveling in hot backseats of cars as the DVD player breaks during an epic traffic jam, or watching a continuous loop of the 24-hour news at a grimy airport—you'll be amusing yourself with the more than 100 peculiar, atypical, goofy, droll, and fun things to do inside this book.

Teach yourself trucker lingo * Play a rousing round of Radio Bingo * Draw squirrels, frogs, and pigeons * Create Eman Sgat for your sdneirf * Go on a digital camera scavenger hunt * Predict your future * Tahk like a movie stahr * Play the Slang Game * And more, much more, and then, even more after that.

All you need is your toothbrush and this book!

Don't Unravel When You Travel will not only keep you busy, but it will also help you entertain the rest of your travel companions. So, what are you waiting for? Grab a pencil and some markers and get ready for the adventure before the adventure.

Hey, if life is a journey, the getting there should be as much fun as being there.

Bon Voyage!

Traffic jam? No problem.

Cancelled flight? Who cares!

Rotten weather?
Don't Unravel When You Travel
has you covered!

Pack It Up & Move It Out

The things you pack in
your luggage for your
vacation may be dictated
by your parents or even by airline restrictions!
Throw caution to the wind—draw what you'd
REALLY like to take along on your holiday.

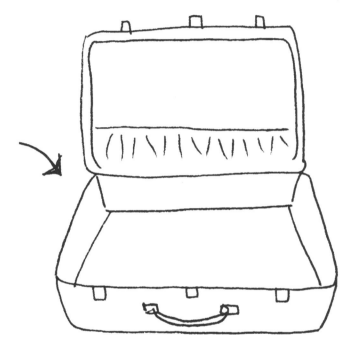

Suggestions:

best friend

14 boxes of candy

computer games

marshmallows

your dog

a lizard . . .

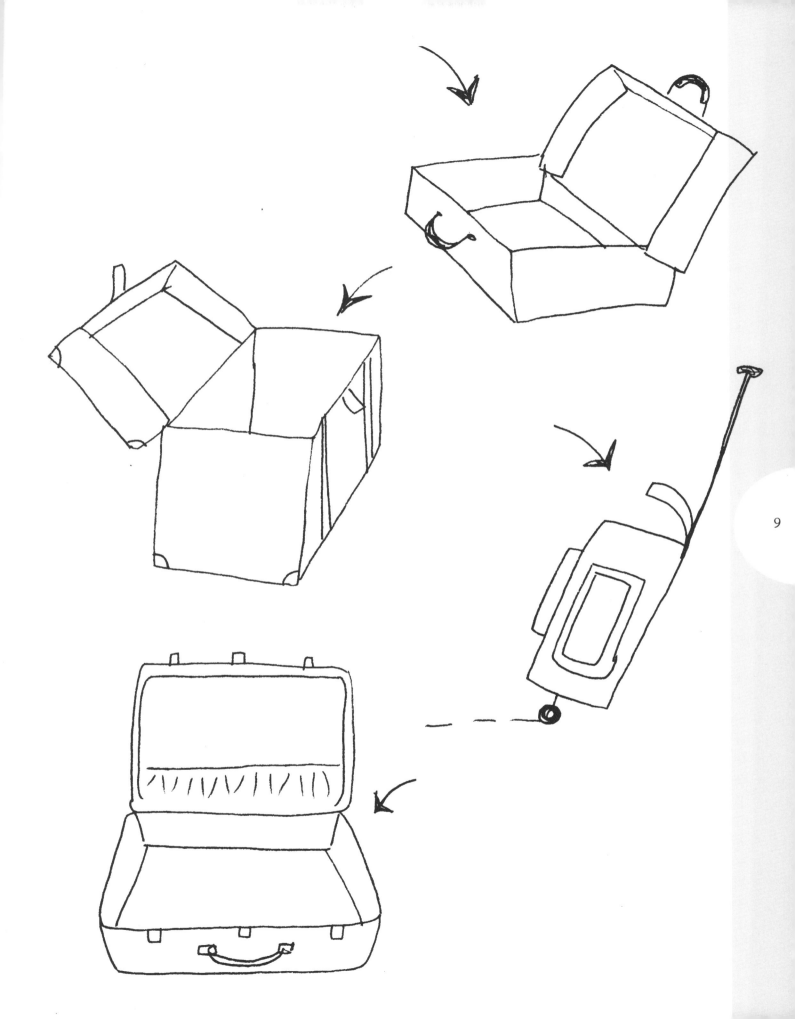

Hinky Pinky

A HINKY PINKY is a riddle with two rhyming words as the answer. *Here's an example:* What's a HINKY PINKY for a noisy bunch of people?

Figure out the following HINKY PINKIES. (They start off easy and get more challenging as you go on.) Answers on page 248.

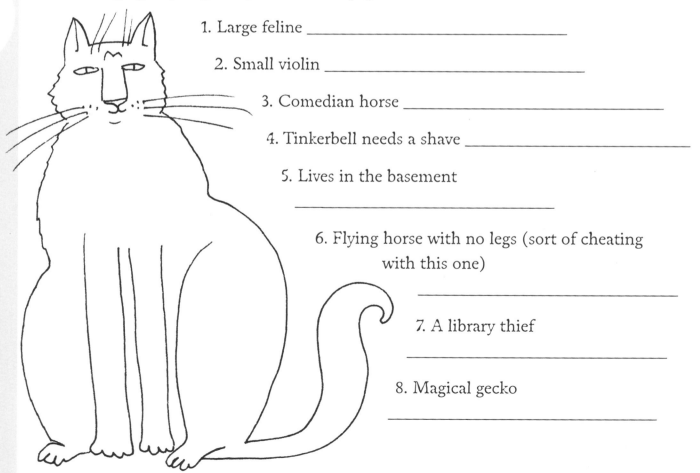

1. Large feline _____

2. Small violin _____

3. Comedian horse _____

4. Tinkerbell needs a shave _____

5. Lives in the basement

_____

6. Flying horse with no legs (sort of cheating with this one)

_____

7. A library thief

_____

8. Magical gecko

_____

9. A sneaky bug _____

10. What baby cats wear on their paws_____

11. A hip ghost _____

12. Rabbit with a sense of humor _____

13. A cool flick _____

14. Sleeping noises that don't excite you _____

15. Used to fix your sole _____

16. Used to weigh very heavy animals _____

17. What you say when a bovine steps on your foot _____

18. A place for Theodore to sleep _____

19. Marching people acting out things without talking (this one's tough!)

_____

20. Burnt money _____

21. Special HINKY PINKY extra-hard one: The White House

_____

TIME TO MAKE UP YOUR OWN!

"I've Got My Eye on You."

Misbehaving in the backseat? Dad might be driving, but he can see everything you're up to in his rearview mirror. And all you can see are his eyes. Draw his eyes depending on what's happening in the car.

Dad needs more coffee.

Dad loves this song.

Dad just got cut off by a minivan.

Dad needs you to stop pinching your sibling...NOW!

"No, we are not there yet!!!!"

Dad has to use the facilities.

Dad's not sure what exit to get off, and
Mom's asleep in the passenger seat.

Make up some of your own!

Dad's been driving for way too long.

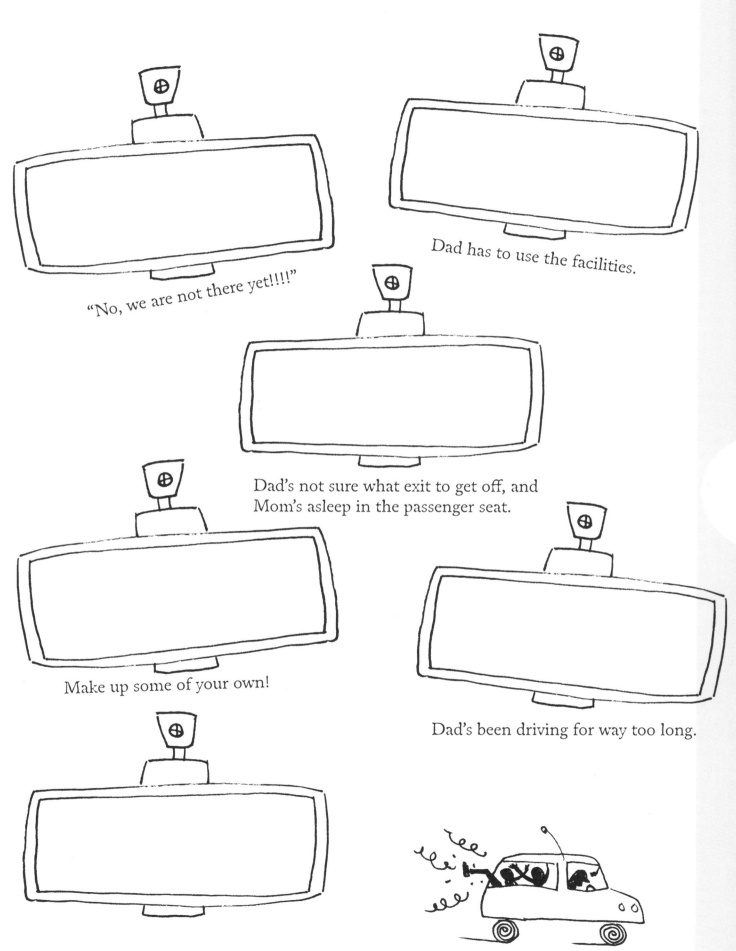

Two Truths & a Lie

Play this game for a round or two before reading the information on page 16. Then play again.

This is an easy game to play on long car trips or when you're stuck on line at an amusement park. Fold and tear out a card for each person playing. (You can also do this "in your head" without any paper and pencils.) Have each player write down two truths about themselves and one statement that's not true (in any order). Whoever goes first then reads her three statements out loud. The other players can each guess the lie separately or they can vote. It's a great way to get to know people you may not know so well (distant cousins) and people you spend all your time with. Who knows what you'll learn!

Two Truths & a Lie about your authors

1. We are actually married!

2. We worked together for several years at the same company.

3. We both have daughters named Margaret Rose.

(See answer on page 248.)

1

2

3

1

2

3

1

2

3

1

2

3

1

2

3

1

2

3

How to Tell if Someone Is Lying

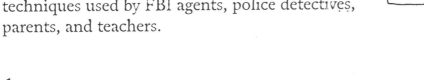

Here are some quick tips to help figure out if someone is lying to you. These are techniques used by FBI agents, police detectives, parents, and teachers.

1   If the speaker doesn't make eye contact, he may be lying.

2   A sudden deep breath may be a sign that a lie has just taken place.

3   If the speaker looks up to the right, he may be lying. Supposedly this stimulates the part of the brain associated with making things up. While looking up to the left stimulates recalling memories or telling the truth. (We're not making this up, though some scientists think this is bunk!)

4   If the speaker touches his nose or covers his mouth, he may be subconsciously "covering up" a lie.

5   If the speaker's voice gets higher or slightly squeaky, this could also be a sign of lying.

6   Look for a fake smile where either the lips move but the eyes don't or the eyes move toward a "happy" expression somewhat after the lips do.

7   Ultimately, if you know the speaker, look for general nervousness. If you're paying attention, you'll see it—your family member or friend will do something that seems unnatural to them. They'll suddenly cross their legs, fidget with their hands, look you straight in the eyes without blinking at all. With some practice, you'll know.

Apply what you have learned and play Two Truths & a Lie on the next page. Are you better at catching a lie now?

1

2

3

1

2

3

1

2

3

1

2

3

1

2

3

1

2

3

OMG

Travel Back in Time with
THE SLANG GAME

This game has three different parts to it. First, for each section, match the slang on the left with its correct meaning on the right. Second, match the decade with each section of slang. Finally, start using these cool, totally awesome, rad sayings all day—or at least until your travel companions make you stop!

DECADES TO CHOOSE FROM:
1890s, 1920s, 1960s, 1980s

Gee whillikers!

Section 1

DECADE:_____

SLANG

1. Take a chill pill
2. Tubular
3. Gag me with a spoon
4. Gnarly
5. Hoser
6. Have a cow
7. Rad
8. Stoked
9. Make my day
10. Like totally

MEANING *of* SLANG

Beyond extreme
I am really hopeful
Awesome
Get overly excited
Loser
Radical
Relax
Don't mess with me
I agree
Disgusting

Section 2

DECADE:_____

SLANG

1. The bee's knees
2. Hard-boiled
3. Spiffy
4. And how!
5. Horsefeathers
6. The big cheese
7. Flapper
8. A pill
9. Heebie-jeebies
10. Putting on the Ritz

MEANING *of* SLANG

Doing something in a grand manner
The boss
Tough
The jitters
Elegant in appearance
I strongly agree
That's nonsense
An unconventional young woman
An unlikable person
The best

Section 3

DECADE:_____

SLANG

1. A gas
2. Flower child
3. Gimme some skin!
4. Heavy
5. Ape
6. Cool it
7. Flake off
8. Groovy
9. Hang it on me again
10. Bummed out

MEANING *of* SLANG

Depressed
Please say that again
Something great
Stop
Deep or cool
Shake my hand
Getting crazy angry over something
Hippie
Go away
A lot of fun

Answers on page 248.

10 Things to Do with Drinking Straws

While on the road, gather as many straws as you can for these time-wasting activities. Most of these can be done in the car, but there's one you'll need some tape for. When at a restaurant always ask your server for straws. She'll probably be happy to give you a bunch as long as you don't launch any spitballs at her. By the way, National Drinking Straw Day is on January 3rd. (It's the anniversary of the day in 1888 that Marvin C. Stone acquired the patent for drinking straws.)

1. Drawing Straws

So, you're at a rest stop in the car, and Junior's stinky diaper needs to be thrown away. Who's going to do it? Simple. Grab one straw for each person in the car (minus Junior). Cut one of the straws so it's smaller than the rest. Put them in your fist and have everyone pick one. The one who gets the short straw dumps the diaper.

2. Bug Catcher

With this contraption, you'll be able to catch some insects at the next rest stop.

WHAT YOU NEED: A clear plastic cup with a lid, 2 straws, and some gum

WHAT TO DO: Place one straw in the hole in the cup lid. Chew some gum for a while and then place it around the hole so no air will get out. Then, poke a small hole in the bottom of the cup and insert the other straw. Chew more gum and seal the hole with it. Go up to a bug, place one straw end just above it and inhale on the other straw. Instant bug vacuum! Check out the bug for a bit and then let him go by popping off the lid and dropping him back where he belongs.

3. Straw Sculptures

Grab as many straws as you can from as many restaurants as you visit. Then, start building whatever you can. To attach the straws, fold the end of one straw into the other.

4. Straw Soccer

Play this one at a restaurant before the drinks arrive at the table. Roll up some small balls from the straw wrappers and with the person across the table from you, blow one ball back and forth until someone scores by getting the ball past the opponent's end of the table. If the game gets too rough, wait till you have more room and a bigger table.

5. Straw Launcher

This one takes a little bit of work, but when you're done, you'll be able to launch a straw into space! Okay, perhaps not space, but definitely up in the air.

WHAT YOU NEED: 2 straws, one slightly smaller than the other; gum (or modeling clay if you have some); empty 20-ounce bottle

WHAT TO DO: Place the smaller straw in the neck of the bottle and seal in place with a big glob of chewed gum. Most of the straw should extend outside of the bottle. Seal one end of the larger straw with a tiny amount of gum and then place this straw over the smaller straw. Find an appropriate launching site (not inside the car) and smash the bottle between your hands. Watch the larger straw fly. If you end up watching a big glob of gum fly instead, wait until you can get your hands on modeling clay.

6. Make a Hoopster

You need some supplies to make this flyer, but it's worth it.

WHAT YOU NEED: straw, tape, scissors, 3 x 5-inch index card

WHAT TO DO: Cut the index card the long way into three equal strips. Create a hoop with one of the pieces and tape the ends together. Tape the other two pieces together end to end. Then make a bigger hoop out of this strip. Tape the hoops to the ends of the straw as shown in the illustration. Make sure they line up. Hold the hoopster by its middle and toss it. Experiment with more straws and more hoops!

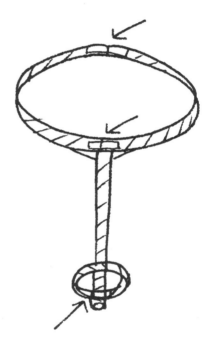

7. No-Sip Straws

At the next restaurant, challenge your sister (or whoever) to drink water from her glass with two straws: one inside the glass and one outside the glass. Have her put both straws in her mouth and sip. She won't be able to drink any water.

8. Stab an Apple

Cover one opening of a straw with your thumb. Thrust the straw into the apple. It will go through as if it were a knife. Try it without covering the opening. Won't work.

When you close one opening of the straw, the air cannot escape from that end. This makes the straw very rigid and increases the air pressure inside. With very little force, the straw goes through the apple.

9. Straw Horn

Flatten one end of a straw and then cut the ends as shown in the illustration. Blow.

10. More Straw Noise

Insert a bendable straw into your armpit with the bendable portion poking up through the neck of your shirt. Blow until you get that unmistakable sound. See figure 1.

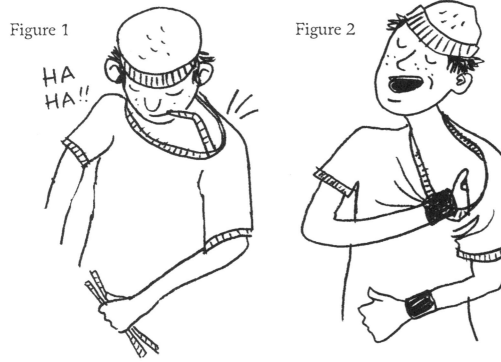

Figure 1

HA HA!!

Figure 2

The same sound can be achieved by grabbing your armpit and pumping your arm up and down as shown in figure 2.

Airport Maze

Have you ever had a dream where you're trying to get some-
where . . . and you're late . . . and you keep getting lost?
That can be what it's like in an airport—only you're carrying
heavy luggage. Navigate this maze and see if you can make
it to your flight before final boarding—in 2 minutes. Check
your route on the answer key on page 249.

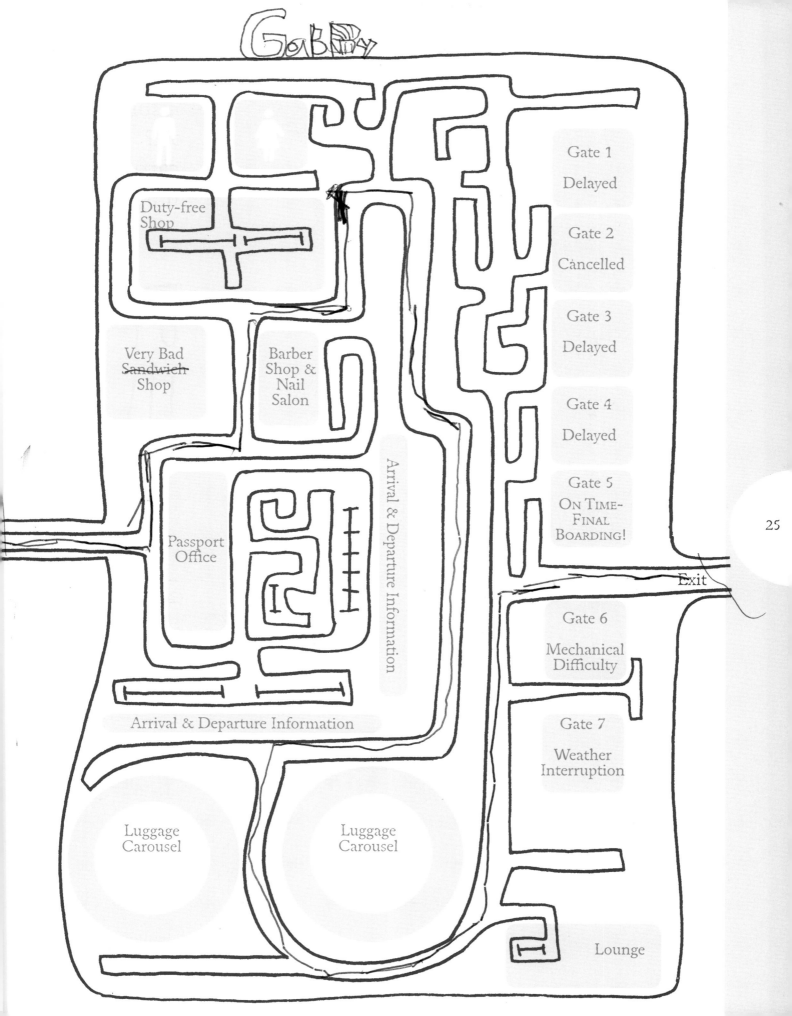

Gabby

Gate 1
Delayed

Gate 2
Cancelled

Gate 3
Delayed

Gate 4
Delayed

Gate 5
ON TIME-
FINAL
BOARDING!

Duty-free
Shop

Very Bad
Sandwich
Shop

Barber
Shop &
Nail
Salon

Passport
Office

Arrival & Departure Information

Arrival & Departure Information

Exit

Gate 6
Mechanical
Difficulty

Gate 7
Weather
Interruption

Luggage
Carousel

Luggage
Carousel

Lounge

Elemental Words

You may not have studied the Periodic Table of the Elements in science class yet, but that doesn't mean you can't start having fun with it now!

Here's the game: Grab a travel mate, with each getting a scorecard. Use the ones provided, or make your own. Give yourselves 15 minutes to come up with as many words as possible using the abbreviations in this table. You can use the abbreviations forward or backward.

For Example:

If you want to spell SCIENCE, you'd use elements 55 (backward), 53, 10 (backward), 58. You get 10 protons for each word created that your competitor doesn't. Whoever has the most protons at the end of 15 minutes is totally nuclear!

You can also play by yourself—just keep trying to find new words!

The Periodic Table is an arrangement of the chemical elements according to their atomic numbers. Atomic numbers are the number of protons in an atomic nucleus. Protons are . . . um . . . space creatures that, um . . . I'll get back to you on this.

H¹																	He²
Li³	Be⁴											B⁵	C⁶	N⁷	O⁸	F⁹	Ne¹⁰
Na¹¹	Mg¹²											Al¹³	Si¹⁴	P¹⁵	S¹⁶	Cl¹⁷	Ar¹⁸
K¹⁹	Ca²⁰	Sc²¹	Ti²²	V²³	Cr²⁴	Mn²⁵	Fe²⁶	Co²⁷	Ni²⁸	Cu²⁹	Zn³⁰	Ga³¹	Ge³²	As³³	Se³⁴	Br³⁵	Kr³⁶
Rb³⁷	Sr³⁸	Y³⁹	Zr⁴⁰	Nb⁴¹	Mo⁴²	Tc⁴³	Ru⁴⁴	Rh⁴⁵	Pd⁴⁶	Ag⁴⁷	Cd⁴⁸	In⁴⁹	Sn⁵⁰	Sb⁵¹	Te⁵²	I⁵³	Xe⁵⁴
Cs⁵⁵	Ba⁵⁶	La⁵⁷	Hf⁷²	Ta⁷³	W⁷⁴	Re⁷⁵	Os⁷⁶	Ir⁷⁷	Pt⁷⁸	Au⁷⁹	Hg⁸⁰	Ti⁸¹	Pb⁸²	Bi⁸³	Po⁸⁴	At⁸⁵	Rn⁸⁶
Fr⁸⁷	Ra⁸⁸	Ac⁸⁹	Unq¹⁰⁴	Unp¹⁰⁵	Unh¹⁰⁶	Uns¹⁰⁷	Uno¹⁰⁸	Une¹⁰⁹	Unn¹¹⁰								

Ce⁵⁸	Pr⁵⁹	Nd⁶⁰	Pm⁶¹	Sm⁶²	Eu⁶³	Gd⁶⁴	Tb⁶⁵	Dy⁶⁶	Ho⁶⁷	Er⁶⁸	Tm⁶⁹	Yb⁷⁰	Lu⁷¹
Th⁹⁰	Pa⁹¹	U⁹²	Np⁹³	Pu⁹⁴	Am⁹⁵	Cm⁹⁶	Bk⁹⁷	Cf⁹⁸	Es⁹⁹	Fm¹⁰⁰	Md¹⁰¹	No¹⁰²	Lr¹⁰³

1. _____

2. _____

3. _____

4. _____

5. _____

6. _____

7. _____

8. _____

9. _____

10. _____

TOTAL Protons:
_____

1. _____

2. _____

3. _____

4. _____

5. _____

6. _____

7. _____

8. _____

9. _____

10. _____

TOTAL Protons:
_____

Geography

The premise of this is simple. Write down a geographical location (town, city, country, continent, body of water, mountain range . . . whatever). Then, write down another place that begins with the last letter of the first place you wrote. Keep going until you run out of places. See if you can fill the page. Have whoever's around help out, and you can even turn this into a game by having everyone take turns.

....

....

....

....

....

....

....

HINT: Watch out for names that begin and end in "A." It works for a minute and then suddenly you're stuck!

World Records

While you may not break any world records in the back of the car (or anywhere), grab a watch and challenge your family and friends to set (and break) the records below!

The Feat	The Winner & Record
Holding breath the longest	
Not blinking the longest	
Most blinking in a minute	
How long you can go without using your thumbs	
How long you can talk without using the letter "E"	
Recite the alphabet fastest	
Everyone eat four crackers—who can whistle first?	
Most spoons stuck on face (for inspiration see page 32)	
Most french fries consumed in 35 seconds	
Make hard candy last the longest (must stay in mouth)	
Most cartwheels in a row	
Most somersaults in a row	

The Feat	The Winner & Record
Most jumping jacks in a row	
Standing on one foot longest	
Holding a note while singing longest	
Most convincing dog bark	
Whistle Dixie the fastest	
Consume soft drink fastest	
Longest belch	
Most convincing ape behavior	
(Come up with your own records)	

Well done!
Congratulations!

Go Ahead, Break Them!

Put your talents to the test. The next truck stop or diner you find yourself in, ask for a handful of metal spoons. You may have to do some fast talking to get that many spoons from the waitress . . .

Balancing Spoons

The most spoons balanced on the face is 16 and was achieved by Joe Allison of the UK. He used stainless steel teaspoons and balanced 5 on the forehead, 4 on the cheeks, 1 on the nose, 2 on his top lip, 1 on each ear, and 2 on the chin.

Here are some tips if you wish to break this record:

• One way to get the spoons to stick to your face is called the rubbing method. Place the concave surface of a spoon up to your nose (might as well start there!). Gently rub the spoon downward. Give it a little bit of pressure when you rub down, but none on the way up. At some point, you'll feel the spoon slightly stick. See if it stays.

• Some people swear by the breath method. Simply breathe on the spoon or lick it a little bit. And then immediately place it on your nose.

• When hanging spoons from your forehead, rub or breathe with the convex side down.

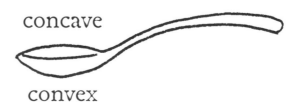
concave

convex

Fast Talkin'

In 1995, Canadian Sean Shannon recited *Hamlet's* "To be or not to be" soliloquy, which is 260 words, in just 23.8 seconds. How long does it take you?

"
To be, or not to be: that is the question:
Whether 'tis nobler in the mind to suffer
The slings and arrows of outrageous fortune,
Or to take arms against a sea of troubles,
And by opposing end them? To die: to sleep;
No more; and by a sleep to say we end
The heart-ache and the thousand natural shocks
That flesh is heir to, 'tis a consummation
Devoutly to be wish'd. To die, to sleep;
To sleep: perchance to dream: ay, there's the rub;
For in that sleep of death what dreams may come
When we have shuffled off this mortal coil,
Must give us pause: there's the respect
That makes calamity of so long life;
For who would bear the whips and scorns of time,
The oppressor's wrong, the proud man's contumely,
The pangs of despised love, the law's delay,
The insolence of office and the spurns
That patient merit of the unworthy takes,
When he himself might his quietus make
With a bare bodkin? Who would fardels bear,
To grunt and sweat under a weary life,
But that the dread of something after death,
The undiscover'd country from whose bourn
No traveller returns, puzzles the will
And makes us rather bear those ills we have
Than fly to others that we know not of?
Thus conscience does make cowards of us all;
And thus the native hue of resolution
Is sicklied o'er with the pale cast of thought,
And enterprises of great pitch and moment
With this regard their currents turn awry,
And lose the name of action.
"

Map Quest

While traveling, it's often nice to stop and think about all you've left behind. Use the space to the right to map what's familiar to you. Pick two spots and map the route. You can map your home to school or your favorite restaurant. From the bathroom to the living room. You decide. Have someone you know do the same map as you and see how close they are when you're finished!

For Example:

This map shows the territory of Roman, the black and white cat.

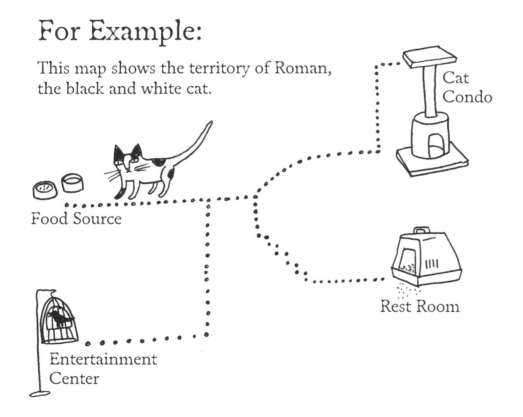

Cat Condo

Food Source

Rest Room

Entertainment Center

The Great Autograph Hunt

As you travel through life (or to Arizona), collect the autographs of the people you meet. BUT (and this is a big but), the names you collect need to follow the rules below (can be first or last names, but most of these will be easier if you're looking for first names):

1 Starts with the letter "E"

....

2 From the Bible (Matthew, Mark, Ruth, Abraham)

....

3 In a familiar song

....

4 Same as yours (not a family member)

....

5 Same as someone in your class

....

6 Same as a US president

....

7 Same as a famous king or queen

....

8 Same as one of the authors of this book

....

9 Has to have at least three vowels

....

10 Name can be broken up into two smaller names (Kaylee, Joanne)

....

11 Rhymes with "bed"

....

12 Is also a common noun (Bill, Rose, Patty, Paige [spelling can be different])

13 Is a month

....

....

14 Can be an adjective (Sandy, Amber)

....

15 Ends in an "a"

....

16 Can be found in nature (Jasmine, River, Willow)

....

17 Is also a place (Dakota, Dallas, Trenton)

....

18 Has an unusual spelling

....

Hitchhikers

Draw some bugs who have come along for the ride.

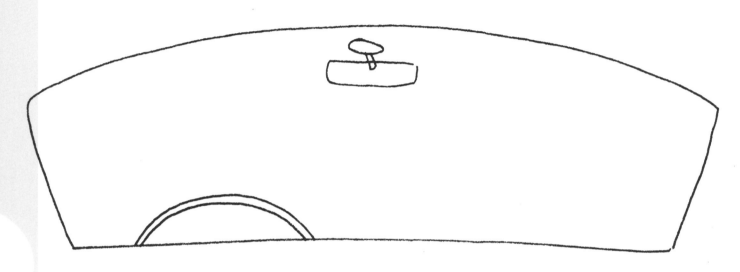

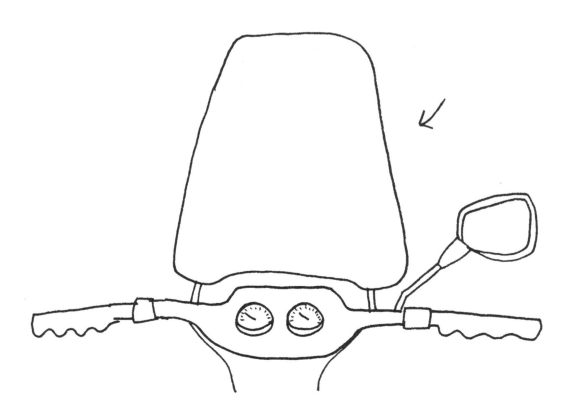

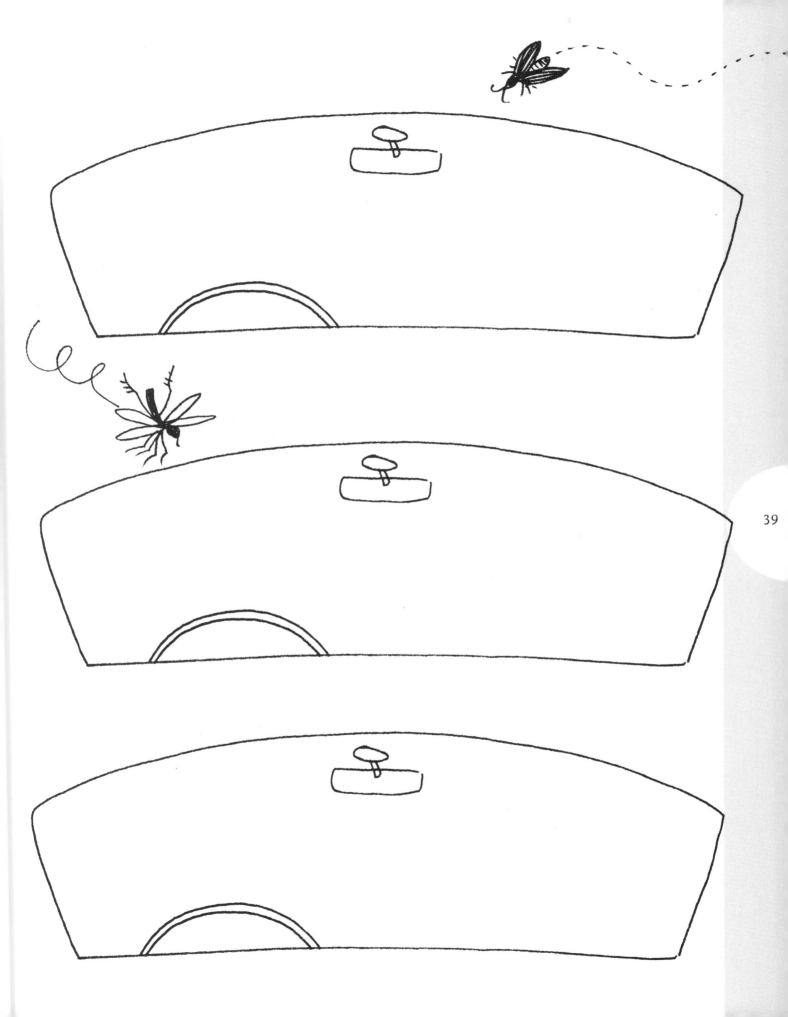

I'm My Own Grandfather

Test how much you know about how people can be related to each other. This will come in handy at the next family reunion. If you have your family nearby, read each sentence out loud and see who can correctly guess what the relation is.

Here's an example:

Who's your father's sister's husband?

ANSWER: Your uncle. (Don't worry, these get harder.)

1   Who's your father's father's father's father?

_____

2   Who's your mother's daughter's son (not your own)?

_____

3   Who's your grandmother's brother?

_____

4   Your father's brother marries your mother's sister and they have two children. Who are they to you?

_____

5 Who's your grandmother's only grandchild?

_____

6 Who's your mother's first cousin's daughter or son?

_____

7 Who's your uncle's mother's mother's husband?

_____

8 Who's your brother's son's sister's mother?

_____

9 Who's your first cousin's son?

_____

10 How could you be your own grandfather?

_____

_____

Now, come up with your own to baffle
your mother's uncle's aunt (whoever that is).

11 _____

12 _____

13 _____

14 _____

15 _____

Find out if you
are your own
grandfather, and
the answers to these
questions on page
249.

Squigglies!

Use these squigglies as beginnings for
your own wonderful drawings.

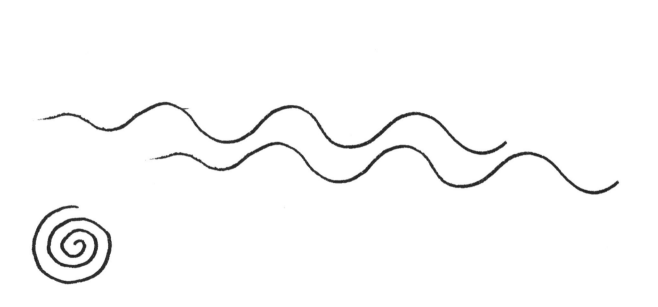

IQ Quiz

Score 5 points for each correct answer.
After you take the quiz,
test your friends.
Be careful!

1 If a rooster laid a white egg and a brown egg, what kinds of chicks would hatch?

YOUR ANSWER: YOUR FRIEND'S ANSWER   ANOTHER FRIEND'S ANSWER:

_____

YOUR SCORE: 5 OR 0   FRIEND'S SCORE: 5 OR 0   ANOTHER FRIEND'S SCORE: 5 OR 0

_____

2 How many animals did Moses take on the ark?

YOUR ANSWER: YOUR FRIEND'S ANSWER   ANOTHER FRIEND'S ANSWER:

_____

YOUR SCORE: 5 OR 0   FRIEND'S SCORE: 5 OR 0   ANOTHER FRIEND'S SCORE: 5 OR 0

_____

3 What would it take to jump higher than a building?

YOUR ANSWER: YOUR FRIEND'S ANSWER   ANOTHER FRIEND'S ANSWER:

_____

YOUR SCORE: 5 OR 0   FRIEND'S SCORE: 5 OR 0   ANOTHER FRIEND'S SCORE: 5 OR 0

_____

4 Which weighs more: a pound of gold or a pound of feathers?

YOUR ANSWER: YOUR FRIEND'S ANSWER   ANOTHER FRIEND'S ANSWER:

_____

YOUR SCORE: 5 OR 0   FRIEND'S SCORE: 5 OR 0   ANOTHER FRIEND'S SCORE: 5 OR 0

_____

5 How much dirt is in a hole 15-feet wide and 6-feet deep?

YOUR ANSWER: YOUR FRIEND'S ANSWER   ANOTHER FRIEND'S ANSWER:

_____

YOUR SCORE: 5 OR 0   FRIEND'S SCORE: 5 OR 0   ANOTHER FRIEND'S SCORE: 5 OR 0

_____

6 A farmer has 28 cows. All but 7 are sold. How many cows does the farmer have left?

YOUR ANSWER: YOUR FRIEND'S ANSWER   ANOTHER FRIEND'S ANSWER:

_____

YOUR SCORE: 5 OR 0   FRIEND'S SCORE: 5 OR 0   ANOTHER FRIEND'S SCORE: 5 OR 0

_____

7 How much is 27 times 45 times 834 times 3 times 9,285 times 0?

YOUR ANSWER: YOUR FRIEND'S ANSWER   ANOTHER FRIEND'S ANSWER:

_____

YOUR SCORE: 5 OR 0   FRIEND'S SCORE: 5 OR 0   ANOTHER FRIEND'S SCORE: 5 OR 0

_____

8 How many months have 28 days?

YOUR ANSWER: YOUR FRIEND'S ANSWER   ANOTHER FRIEND'S ANSWER:

_____

YOUR SCORE: 5 OR 0   FRIEND'S SCORE: 5 OR 0   ANOTHER FRIEND'S SCORE: 5 OR 0

_____

9 A 10-foot rope ladder hangs over the side of a boat with the bottom rung on the surface of the water. The rungs are 1 foot apart, and the tide goes up at the rate of 6 inches per hour. How long will it be until three rungs are covered?

YOUR ANSWER: YOUR FRIEND'S ANSWER   ANOTHER FRIEND'S ANSWER:

_____

YOUR SCORE: 5 OR 0   FRIEND'S SCORE: 5 OR 0   ANOTHER FRIEND'S SCORE: 5 OR 0

_____

10 You only have one match when you enter a dark and cold room. You come across an oil lamp, an oil heater, and a candle. Which do you light first?

YOUR ANSWER: YOUR FRIEND'S ANSWER   ANOTHER FRIEND'S ANSWER:

_____

YOUR SCORE: 5 OR 0   FRIEND'S SCORE: 5 OR 0   ANOTHER FRIEND'S SCORE: 5 OR 0

_____

11 How can the 48th and 50th U.S. Presidents have the same parents, but not be brothers?

YOUR ANSWER: YOUR FRIEND'S ANSWER   ANOTHER FRIEND'S ANSWER:

_____

YOUR SCORE: 5 OR 0   FRIEND'S SCORE: 5 OR 0   ANOTHER FRIEND'S SCORE: 5 OR 0

_____

12 What is the eleven-letter word that all college graduates spell incorrectly?

YOUR ANSWER: YOUR FRIEND'S ANSWER   ANOTHER FRIEND'S ANSWER:

_____

YOUR SCORE: 5 OR 0   FRIEND'S SCORE: 5 OR 0   ANOTHER FRIEND'S SCORE: 5 OR 0

_____

13 If you spell "sit all day in the tub" S-O-A-K, and you spell "a funny story" J-O-K-E, how do you spell "the white of an egg"?

YOUR ANSWER: YOUR FRIEND'S ANSWER   ANOTHER FRIEND'S ANSWER:

YOUR SCORE: 5 OR 0   FRIEND'S SCORE: 5 OR 0   ANOTHER FRIEND'S SCORE: 5 OR 0

14 Why are 2010 pennies worth more than 2009 pennies?

YOUR ANSWER: YOUR FRIEND'S ANSWER   ANOTHER FRIEND'S ANSWER:

YOUR SCORE: 5 OR 0   FRIEND'S SCORE: 5 OR 0   ANOTHER FRIEND'S SCORE: 5 OR 0

15 How far can you walk into the woods?

YOUR ANSWER: YOUR FRIEND'S ANSWER   ANOTHER FRIEND'S ANSWER:

YOUR SCORE: 5 OR 0   FRIEND'S SCORE: 5 OR 0   ANOTHER FRIEND'S SCORE: 5 OR 0

16 A plane crashes on the United States-Canada border. In which country are the survivors buried?

YOUR ANSWER: YOUR FRIEND'S ANSWER   ANOTHER FRIEND'S ANSWER:

YOUR SCORE: 5 OR 0   FRIEND'S SCORE: 5 OR 0   ANOTHER FRIEND'S SCORE: 5 OR 0

17 Why is it against the law for a man living in North Carolina to be buried in South Carolina?

YOUR ANSWER: YOUR FRIEND'S ANSWER   ANOTHER FRIEND'S ANSWER:

YOUR SCORE: 5 OR 0   FRIEND'S SCORE: 5 OR 0   ANOTHER FRIEND'S SCORE: 5 OR 0

18 Henry's mother had four children. The first was April, the second was May, and the third was June. What was the name of her fourth child?

YOUR ANSWER: YOUR FRIEND'S ANSWER   ANOTHER FRIEND'S ANSWER:

YOUR SCORE: 5 OR 0   FRIEND'S SCORE: 5 OR 0   ANOTHER FRIEND'S SCORE: 5 OR 0

19 What are tree mistake in this sentence?

YOUR ANSWER: YOUR FRIEND'S ANSWER   ANOTHER FRIEND'S ANSWER:

YOUR SCORE: 5 OR 0   FRIEND'S SCORE: 5 OR 0   ANOTHER FRIEND'S SCORE: 5 OR 0

20 There are 5 apples in a basket and 5 people in a room. How can you give an apple to each person in the room and yet leave one apple in the basket.

YOUR ANSWER: YOUR FRIEND'S ANSWER   ANOTHER FRIEND'S ANSWER:

YOUR SCORE: 5 OR 0   FRIEND'S SCORE: 5 OR 0   ANOTHER FRIEND'S SCORE: 5 OR 0

21 If there are 24 apples and you take away 3, how many apples do you have?

YOUR ANSWER: YOUR FRIEND'S ANSWER   ANOTHER FRIEND'S ANSWER:

YOUR SCORE: 5 OR 0   FRIEND'S SCORE: 5 OR 0   ANOTHER FRIEND'S SCORE: 5 OR 0

22 You're walking down the street and you see a one-story green house. You go in and everything is green. The walls are green, the floor is green, and the furniture is green. Even the cat is green. What color are the stairs?

YOUR ANSWER: YOUR FRIEND'S ANSWER   ANOTHER FRIEND'S ANSWER:

_____

YOUR SCORE: 5 OR 0   FRIEND'S SCORE: 5 OR 0   ANOTHER FRIEND'S SCORE: 5 OR 0

_____

23 You're flying a plane from Florida to Oregon at 200 miles per hour. The flight goes well for the first few hours. Then the plane runs out of gas and crashes in Colorado. Who crashed the plane?

YOUR ANSWER: YOUR FRIEND'S ANSWER   ANOTHER FRIEND'S ANSWER:

_____

YOUR SCORE: 5 OR 0   FRIEND'S SCORE: 5 OR 0   ANOTHER FRIEND'S SCORE: 5 OR 0

_____

24 You have two U.S. coins. Together you have 30 cents. One of the coins is not a nickel. What are the coins?

YOUR ANSWER: YOUR FRIEND'S ANSWER   ANOTHER FRIEND'S ANSWER:

_____

YOUR SCORE: 5 OR 0   FRIEND'S SCORE: 5 OR 0   ANOTHER FRIEND'S SCORE: 5 OR 0

_____

25 An electric train is moving north at 100 mph and a wind is blowing to the west at 10 mph. Which way does the smoke blow?

YOUR ANSWER: YOUR FRIEND'S ANSWER   ANOTHER FRIEND'S ANSWER:

_____

YOUR SCORE: 5 OR 0   FRIEND'S SCORE: 5 OR 0   ANOTHER FRIEND'S SCORE: 5 OR 0

_____

ANSWERS ON PAGE 250.

Now That's a Museum!

Ever get tired of visiting museums? Hmm . . . now what would happen if you had the chance to collect items for your very own museum? Well, now's your chance!

Ghost

The object of this game is to avoid getting caught spelling out a word.

1 Begin with one player saying a letter out loud. The next player thinks of a word that begins with that letter and says the second letter in the word.

2 Players take turns adding a letter to the end of the chain as long as the new letter can still be part of a longer word but doesn't complete a word. For example, the first player starts with an "F." The second follows with "A." Then the third player, thinking of the word "fantastic," wants to say "N" but realizes that would spell a word (fan). That player then decides the word will be "favor," so he adds a "V" to the chain.

3 If someone adds a letter that doesn't sound like it can form a word, another player can issue a challenge. If the player who added the letter can't name a word with the letter, she is a ghost (out of the game). So, for example, after the player in step two adds a "V" to "FA", the next player decides to add a "Z." Good time to issue a challenge.

4 You also become a ghost if you have to finish a word or if you mistakenly spell out a shorter word in the process of trying to spell a longer word. For example, if you wanted to spell "favorite" but you become a ghost once you get to "favor."

5 For a longer version of this game, don't count players out when they make a mistake. Simply give them a "g," then an "h" and so on. The last person to spell out "g-h-o-s-t" wins.

Buzz

This is a fun counting game that takes some thought and teamwork.

1 Get as many people to play as possible. The first person begins by counting "one." The next person says "two" and so on. But, every time a player reaches a number that has a seven in it (7, 17, 27, etc.) or is a multiple of seven (7, 14, 21, 28, etc.) she has to say "Buzz" instead of the number.

2 Normally in this game, if a person messes up, he's out. However, you can also play to see how high you can count as a group.

3 There are a couple of different variations to this game. Fizz-Buzz is just like Buzz, except that you say "Fizz" when you reach a number with five in it or is a multiple of five. In Fuzz-Buzz, you also say "Fuzz" when you get to threes and multiples of three.

4 Keep track of the highest number reached without a mistake and who was in the group that reached it.

BUZZ

Highest count reached: _____

Who helped: _____

FIZZ-BUZZ

Highest count reached: _____

Who helped: _____

FUZZ-BIZZ

Highest count reached: _____

Who helped: _____

BUZZ!

FUZZ!

FIZZ!

As Supreme Leader of the mini-van, I promise to stop at rest stops and knick-knack shops, buy candy for everyone and you will be encouraged to jump on the furniture in all hotel rooms!!!

Supreme Ruler of the Car

Don't you think it's time to choose the ruler of the car or plane or vacation location? Ask for nominees and hold an election!

Each person must fill out the following form with as much humor and ridiculousness as possible! Use the blank pages at the end of the book for other nominees.

After filling out the forms, the nominees must read their speeches to the rest of the car, plane, or vacation location. Once all the speeches have been given, hold an election in which no one can vote for themselves.

List of nominees:

_____

_____

_____

_____

_____

THE WINNER IS: _____!!!!!

YOUR NAME: _____

NAME OF YOUR POLITICAL PARTY: _____

YOUR PLATFORM (list of incredible promises you'll never keep once you're elected):

_____

_____

_____

_____

LAWS YOU WILL PASS: _____

_____

_____

_____

SCANDAL THAT WILL FORCE YOU TO STEP DOWN SOON AFTER YOU'RE ELECTED:

_____

_____

Draft your nomination speech here:

Radio Bingo

You know how to play Bingo, right!? With this game, instead of someone calling out a number, turn the radio dial to random stations. If you hear something that's on your sheet, cross it out.

Whoever gets a line across, down, or diagonally wins the first round. Whoever completes the whole board first, wins the second round. Decide ahead of time what the prizes are (M&Ms, the preferred seat in the car, and more!). If the game lasts longer than the car ride, continue it once you get where you're going.

Ad for cell phone company	Mention of a website	Yelling	A song older than you	Someone speaking in a language different from yours
Love song	News	News report from another country	Song that begins with drumming	Voice of a celebrity (not the DJ or a musician)
Song about driving	Song where the singer repeats the title at least seven times	☆ ☆ FREE	Any sort of countdown	Nature sound
Talk show	Contest announcement	Announcement of a big sale	Ad for any kind of food	Mention of a TV show
A blues song	Classical song	A sports show	DJ making a mistake	Station identification

List of upcoming concerts	A break-up song	A politician	News report from another country	Weather bulletin
Someone on the phone	Punk rock song	Silly sound effect	Cola ad	News of a big sale
Talk show	Song with no words (not classical)	FREE	Traffic update	Ad with annoying jingle
Song that begins with saxophone	NPR member station	Ad for a movie	A jazz song	Mention of a TV show
Ad for a car dealership	A song older than you	List of upcoming concerts	Song from a movie	Station identification

Heavy metal song	Ad for any sort of food	DJ giving the time	Any sort of countdown	Man and woman talking
Song that starts off slow and speeds up	A politician	Yelling	Voice of a celebrity	Someone requesting a song
Clapping	Classical song	FREE	Weather	Ad for a lawyer
An apology song	DJ making a mistake	News update	Song about driving	Someone speaking in a different language
Laughing	Rap song	Mention of a website	Cola ad	A sports show

Song that starts with singing before instruments	Country song	List of upcoming concerts	A politician	Rush Limbaugh
An apology song	Song from a movie	Weather update	Man and woman talking	Beatles song
News	Ad with annoying jingle	FREE	DJ giving the time	News report from another country
A break up song	Song with no words	Female DJ	NPR member station	A song older than you
Clapping	Classical song	Nature sound	DJ making a mistake	Traffic update

Silly sound effect	Mention of a website	Country song	Contest	Someone on the phone
Voice of a celebrity	Song with the word "love" in it	Ad for a car dealership	Laughing	Sports show
Any sort of countdown	Weather update	FREE	Ad for any kind of food	Punk Rock Song
Song that starts with guitar playing	Talk show	Heavy Metal Song	Ad for upcoming concert	Yelling
Rap song	Nature sound	Classical song	DJ making a mistake	Someone requesting a song

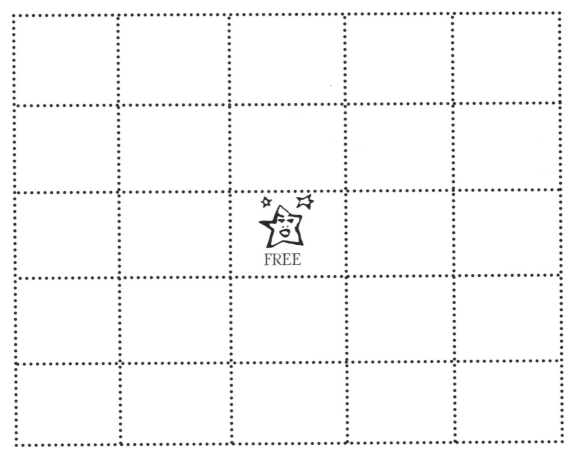

When you've used up all your game boards, use the blank boards to make up your own bingo games. Try Roadside Bingo or Silly-Things-Adults-Say Bingo!

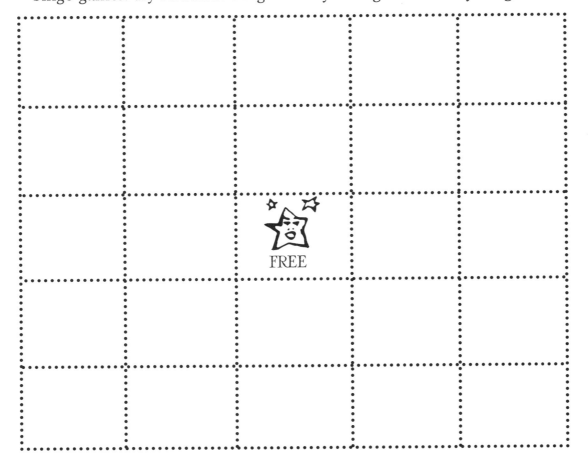

Fairy Tales in the News

What fairy tales inspired these news headlines?
Create illustrations to go with the headlines.
Answers on page 250.

Ball Ends in Chaos as Beautiful Stranger Flees

Prince despondent. Claims he's found his true love . . . but forgot to ask her name!

Your answer: _____

Giant Carnivore Terrorizes Family

See page 22 to read about Grandmother's remarkable recovery.

Your answer: _____

Toy Maker Claims Puppet as Son

Delusional man sent for psychiatric testing.

Your answer: _____

Lost Princess Finds True Love AND
Sues Future Mother-in-Law for Mistreatment

"She made me sleep on 32 mattresses. I turned over and nearly fell to my death!"

Your answer: _____

Siblings Escape Cannibal!

People eater cooked!

Your answer: _____

Daring Prince Kisses 100-year-old Princess

Prince says, "Um . . . it was a nice kiss, but there was an awful lot of dust."

Your answer: _____

Girl Charged with Breaking & Entering

Mr. Bear will drop charges if reparations are made.

Your answer: _____

Woman Claims Baked Goods Ran Away

"If only she didn't peek," says husband.

Your answer: _____

Boy Trades Cow for Paltry Sum

Concocts ludicrous story about really big plant . . . among other things.

Your answer: _____

Long-Haired Woman Seeks Rescue from Tower

"My tears cure blindness and I'm a good cook."

Your answer: _____

Now make up one of your own:

Fairy Tales . . .

. . . have existed for thousands of years. Every culture in the world has its folklore and fairy tales. Many of the same themes overlap, such as witches, enchantments, talking animals, and fantastic happenings. The older stories were intended more for adults, but over time, they have become children's stories.

Eman Sgat

Don't you think that everyone should know their names backwards? You can perform a public service by telling your friends, family members, schoolmates, and people you meet in your travels what their names are backwards. Use the name tags below to fill in the backward names.
You can even cut them out and give them as gifts.
Just take it from Eoj Nagitahr and Nasus Edirbcm, this is fun!

O L L E H
ym eman si

O L L E H
ym eman si

Odranoel Ad IcniV,

otherwise known as LEONARDO DA VINCI, wrote backward in his notebooks. This technique is known as mirror writing, and supposedly, only around .02% of us can do it easily. There are many theories as to why Da Vinci wrote this way, although no one knows for sure. Our favorite theory is that since he was left-handed, he could write from right to left without smudging what he wrote with his hand. This was way before ballpoint pens, remember, and his writing hand would have smeared the ink as the hand moved across the page. Ask any lefty about this—it's annoying!

Give mirror writing a try. It sort of messes with your brain.

67

O L L E H
ym eman si

O L L E H
ym eman si

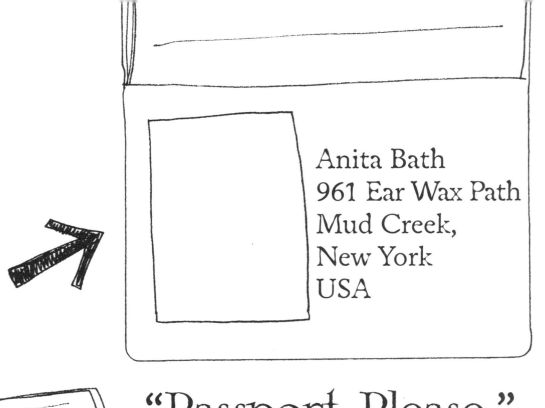

Anita Bath
961 Ear Wax Path
Mud Creek,
New York
USA

"Passport, Please."

There's an old saying that goes something like this: "When you start to look like your passport photo, it's time to go home." Draw the passport photos below using the names and addresses as clues.

Rolf Panter
34 Man's Best
Friend Lane
Whisker City,
Wyoming
USA

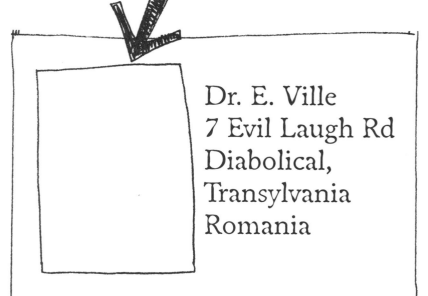

Dr. E. Ville
7 Evil Laugh Rd
Diabolical,
Transylvania
Romania

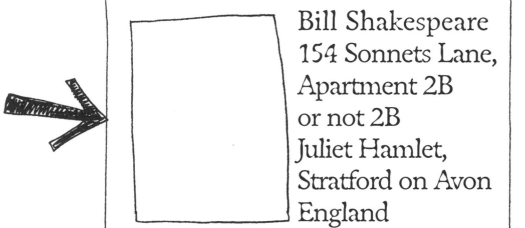

Bill Shakespeare
154 Sonnets Lane,
Apartment 2B
or not 2B
Juliet Hamlet,
Stratford on Avon
England

Barry Gross
99 Pickens Lane
Lizards Innards,
Arizona
USA

PASSPORT

Trucker Lingo

Check out at all the trucks on the road when you travel. They're crisscrossing the country carrying food and merchandise. Truckers communicate with each other using what's called a CB radio. They even have their own lingo.

10-4, good neighbor!

Detail (decorate) these big rigs!

Check out the words and phrases below, and see if you can match them up with their definitions. Once you've figured them out, use these phrases in normal conversation. "Hey Dad, watch out for that alligator on the road!"

1. Granny Lane   A tailgating car

2. Alligator   A small car

3. Double Nickel   A rest stop

4. Plain Wrapper   The slow lane

5. Super Slab   A tollbooth

6. Cash Register   Heavy traffic or a truck carrying cars

7. Clean Shot   55 miles per hour

8. Blue Slip   Slow down

9. Pit Stop   The trucker you're talking to

10. Roger or 10-4   Drive faster

11. Hammer Down   No police ahead

12. Bear   An unmarked police car

13. Antler Alley   A blown tire on the road

14. Parking Lot   A deer crossing

15. Back Off the Hammer!   CB radio nickname

16. Handle   Okay or message received

17. Too Many Eggs in the Basket   The highway

18. A Roller Skate   A police officer

19. Good Neighbor   Traffic ticket

20. A Bumper Sticker   A truck is overweight

Check your answers for Trucker Lingo on page 250.

Spot the Tourists

Travel enthusiasts sometimes stand out in a crowd.
Their curiosity, difference in culture, clothes, and manner can
even make them a spectacle! See how many tourists you can
spot in the illustration below.

Answers on page 251.

How to Draw a Pigeon

Pigeons are also known as Rock Doves. They have aided in communication during times of war as carrier pigeons and have been called flying rats by their detractors. People who love them, feed them daily. They are also on the menu in many French restaurants—known as Squab. No matter how you feel about them, draw in as many as you can in this plaza.

1 2 3 4 5

Follow these 5 simple steps and voila! A pigeon!

GIGANTIC
Digital Camera Scavenger Hunt

Challenge yourself and the rest of your family to take pictures of the following items as you travel to your destination. The person with the most photos wins! Don't forget to take pictures of the attractions as well!

At a Rest Stop

1. Picnic table
2. Woman's room sign
3. Person walking dog
4. Trucker wearing baseball cap
5. Vending machine
6. Discarded diaper
7. Grass
8. Motorcycle
9. Car with travel bubble on top (not yours)
10. Vehicle with more than four wheels
11. Car with bikes on back
12. Maps
13. Water fountain
14. Sports car
15. Crack in the sidewalk

At a Gas Station

1. Cola bottle or can on ground
2. Squeegy for cleaning windshield
3. Squashed gum on ground
4. Oil stain
5. Unleaded Premium gas price
6. Overfilled garbage can
7. Diesel fuel
8. Air machine (for filling tires)
9. Someone stretching
10. Local newspaper
11. Graffiti
12. Tobacco outlet sign
13. Candy wrapper
14. Person with a beard
15. Really dirty windshield

At a Museum

(If you're allowed to take pictures)

1. Velvet ropes

2. Something on the wrong shelf at the gift shop

3. Door that says "No Admittance"

4. Scratchy carpet

5. Tired/bored child

6. Talking display

7. Small child on parent's back

8. Marble floor

9. Full elevator

10. Something purple

11. Yellow backpack

12. Closed-off area

13. Staircase

14. Bones

15. Restroom

At the Zoo or Aquarium

1. Animal that doesn't belong (a squirrel, for instance)

2. Ants

3. Animal butt

4. Sleeping animal

5. Display with no animal to be seen

6. Animal being fed

7. Family getting picture taken

8. Closed display

9. French fries

10. Ketchup packet

11. Someone wearing a hat

12. Bench

13. Someone wearing very loud colors

14. Person with a map

15. Child with face pressed up against the glass

Well, hello there . . .

Gigantic Digital Camera Scavenger Hunt

At the Airport

1. Plane with propellers

2. Airline personnel with luggage

3. Luggage with wheels

4. Bookstore

5. Duty-free shop

6. Starbucks coffee shop

7. Someone running like crazy

8. Arrivals/Departures screen

9. A really long line

10. Person sitting/sleeping on the floor

11. Person on computer

12. Luggage cart

13. Moving sidewalk

14. Motorized cart with elderly passengers

15. Family with at least five children

On the Airplane

1. Crying baby

2. Barf bag

3. In-flight magazine

4. Clouds

5. Smiling flight attendant

6. Someone having trouble closing overhead compartment

7. Bag of peanuts

8. Line for bathroom

9. Tiny bathroom sink

10. Person sleeping

11. Person reading book

12. Drink cart

13. Picture from window of ground

14. The pilot

15. Emergency exit

At the Beach

1. Striped umbrella

2. Beach ball

3. Huge wave

4. Surfer or boogie boarder

5. Lifeguard with white stuff on nose

6. Seashell

7. Seashell with creature still in it

8. Boat

9. Buoy

10. Frisbee

11. Sea bird

12. Driftwood or sea glass

13. Person wearing big hat

14. Person buried in sand

15. Person fishing

At the Family Reunion

1. A second cousin

2. Barbecue

3. Picture of two cousins who have met for the first time

4. Oldest person in attendance

5. Youngest person in attendance

6. Someone not related

7. Half eaten hot dog

8. Sleeping uncle

9. Aunt with crazy hairdo

10. Potato salad

11. Picnic table

12. Lighter fluid for barbecue

13. Blue cooler

14. Folding chair

15. Big cake

Gigantic Digital Camera Scavenger Hunt

In a Foreign Country

1. Sign in a different language

2. Fire hydrant

3. Taxi

4. Water fountain

5. Outdoor market

6. Concierge

7. Outdoor statue

8. Pharmacy

9. Funky looking mannequin

10. Car dealership

11. Candy store

12. Bus or trolley

13. Train station

14. Performance artist

15. Castle or mansion

At the Campsite

1. An RV hookup

2. An eight-person tent

3. A reptile

4. Trail marker

5. Person hiking with walking stick

6. Poison ivy, sumac, or oak

7. An RV towing a car

8. Mountain biker with mud all over her

9. Fire circle

10. Public shower

11. Campsite office

12. Park ranger

13. Beef jerky

14. Lost item of clothing

15. Dog

At the Hotel/Motel

1. Ice maker

2. Vending machines

3. Pool

4. Newspaper

5. Brochure display

6. Key or key card

7. Gideon's Bible

8. Unopened hotel soap

9. Workout room

10. Office door

11. Iron

12. Heat/air conditioning unit

13. Doorman/woman

14. Name of elevator manufacturer (is it Otis?)

15. Waffle maker

Stop jumping on that bed!!!

Total number of points is 165. How did you do?

HAND GAMES from Around the World

Hand games are great for when you're stuck in a seat belt or otherwise not allowed to get up and run around. These games may seem simple, but if you play them enough, you may develop some strategies that help you outwit your opponents.

Rock, Paper, Scissors

This game is played just about everywhere, but some think it has its origins in China.

NUMBER OF PLAYERS: 2 or more

1 Two or more players face each other (as best as you can if you're in a car). The players make a fist and count to three together, each time raising the fist.

2 Then you say, "Shoot!" and turn your fist into one of three weapons below:

—ROCK: a fist

—PAPER: open hand with fingers together

—SCISSORS: index and middle fingers extended and separated (like a pair of scissors)

3 The object is to pick a weapon that defeats the opponent's. How does that work?

EASY:

Rock breaks scissors—rock wins

Scissors cuts paper—scissors wins

Paper covers rock—paper wins.

4 If players choose the same gesture, it's a do over. Play best out of three.

Jan, Ken, Pon

This Indonesian version of Rock, Paper, Scissors has the same rules, but different weapons and gestures.

NUMBER OF PLAYERS: 2 or more

Indonesia . . .

. . . is a country in Southeast Asia (below India and China and north of Australia) that consists of more than 17,500 islands. With a population of more than 230 million people, it's the fourth most populous country in the world. Indonesia has vast areas of wilderness that support the world's second highest level of biodiversity.

1 First off, you say "Jan, Ken, Pon" instead of counting to three as you prepare to attack.

2 Your weapons include an earwig or ant, a human, and an elephant. Here are the gestures:

—EARWIG OR ANT: extended pinky (beats the elephant by crawling into its trunk and driving it insane)

—HUMAN: extended forefinger (beats the earwig by stepping on it)

—ELEPHANT: extended thumb (beats the human by stepping on him).

Morra

This game is played in Spain and Italy, but it actually goes back thousands of years to ancient Greek and Roman times.

NUMBER OF PLAYERS: 2

1 On the count of three, each player throws out one hand with zero to five fingers showing.

2 As you do this, you must each call out your guess as to what the sum of all the fingers will be.

3 If one player guesses correctly, she earns a point. The first player to reach three points wins.

Wan, Tu, Zum

Ready for some confusing fun! This Malaysian game is a more challenging version of Rock, Paper, Scissors.

NUMBER OF PLAYERS: 2 or more

1 Each player starts off with a fist and counts off saying, "bird, rock, pistol, plank, water."

2 They then make one of the following five signs:

BIRD: all five fingers bunched together at the fingertips

ROCK: fist

PISTOL: outstretched thumb and index finger

PLANK: palm facing down

WATER: palm facing up

Malaysia . . .

. . . is located north of Indonesia. It has a diverse population of 27 million and has a tropical climate. If you ever get the opportunity to eat at a Malaysian restaurant, do not pass it up! The food of Malaysia is not to be missed.

3 Here's how you decide who wins: Bird beats plank and water. Rock beats bird, plank, and water. Pistol beats everything except for water. Plank beats bird and water. Water beats everything except bird and plank.

Hipitoi

This two-player game is played by the native Maori of New Zealand, who place great value on quickness and agility. This game is best played standing up, but you can try it sitting as well.

NUMBER OF PLAYERS: 2

1 The object of this game is to anticipate and mimic the leader's hand gesture. Choose a leader, and face each other with fists outstretched and palms touching.

2 The leader utters the traditional challenge, "Hipitoi!" The follower accepts the challenge by saying, "Ra!"

3 The leader chants "hipitoi" while quickly making one of the following hand gestures, which the follower (without hesitation) tries to mimic.

Here are the gestures:

— Two thumbs up

— Two thumbs down

— Right thumb up, left thumb down

— Left thumb up, right thumb down.

4 If the follower fails to match the leader's gesture, no points are awarded, and the follower becomes the leader. The new leader says "Hipitoi!" while quickly making a new hand gesture.

5 If the follower matches the leader's gesture, he wins a point and becomes the leader. However, the other player can block the point by yelling "Ra!" before the new leader can *start* chanting "hipitoi" and making a new hand gesture. So, the new leader has to move very quickly.

6 If the new follower yells "Ra!" first, he gets the point and reclaims the leader position. The other player loses his newly earned point. The first person to get five points wins.

Compete to Eat

Who will win this pie-eating contest? Fill the bellies
of our contestants with as much pie as they can hold—
don't overlap the pieces. Time limit is 10 minutes.
Do this drawing activity with a friend.

Word Gridlock

The object of this game is to score the most points by forming words in your grid. Cut or rip out the game boards and pass them out to anyone who wants to play. When you run out, create your own!

To play, first choose a player to go first. That player calls out any letter, and all the players write that letter into one of the squares on their grid. Moving clockwise, the next player then calls out a letter (which may be the same as or different from any letter already called out. Each player then writes that letter into one of the remaining squares. Once all the letters are filled in, each player writes down every word they can find in their grid. You can find words going across, up and down, backwards, and diagonally. No names or other proper nouns allowed.

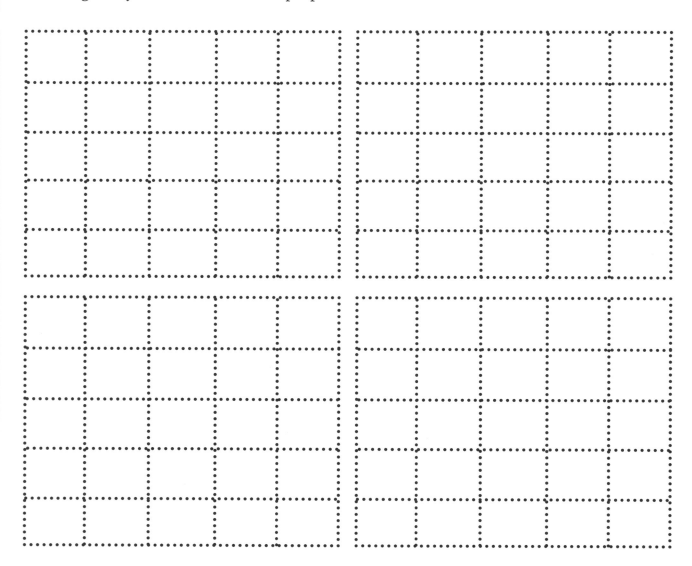

SCORING:
Five-letter word = five points
Four-letter word = four points
Three-letter word = three points

The player with the highest total score wins.

Signs, Signs, Everywhere . . .

Advertise your own business, promote your special skills, make up your own menu, or create a billboard for your uncle, the dentist. Hey, it pays to advertise!

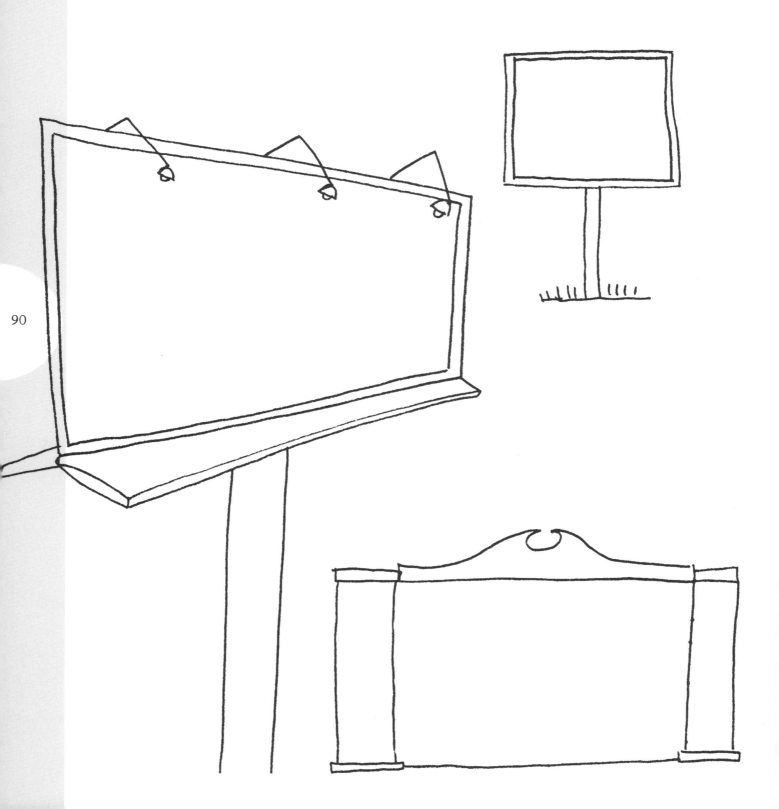

Find the Hidden Animals

There's an amazing song by musician Billy Jonas called, "What Kind of Cat Are You?" In it, he sings about all the different words and phrases cats hide in. For example, What kind of cat hangs out in your house? Give up?

HOUSE CAT!

So, here's a quiz, brought to you by Billy from his song, as well as from the song's sequel: "What Kind of Dog Are You?" These start off easy but get challenging! Answers on page 251.

1. What kind of cat is really, really scared?

_____

2. What kind of cat hangs out at the copy shop?

_____

3. What kind of cat is a big expensive car?

_____

4. What kind of cat is a great big disaster?

_____

5. What kind of cat comes in the mail?

_____

6. What kind of cat is a whole bunch of cows?

_____

7. What kind of cat throws stuff over the wall of a castle?

_____

8. What kind of cat tunnels under the castle?

_____

9. What kind of cat takes a picture of the inside of your body?

_____

10. What kind of cat carries your golf clubs?

_____

11. What kind of dog carries your leftover dinner?

_____

12. What kind of dog sits around the neck of a soldier?

_____

13. What kind of dog sits on a bun at a picnic?

_____

14. What kind of cow do you sit on in your living room?

_____

15. What kind of cow helps you do your taxes?

_____

16. What kind of cow is really, really scared?

_____

17. What kind of yak floats down a river?

_____

18. What kind of yak is crazy and lives in Maine?

_____

19. What kind of yak has trouble sleeping at night?

_____

20. What kind of pig grows out of the back of your head?

_____

21. What kind of pig carries you when you're tired?

_____

22. What kind of pig alks tay ike lay is thay?

_____

23. What kind of bee was just born?

_____

24. What kind of bee could be yes or no?

_____

25. What kind of bee is plastic and flies through the air?

_____

Thanks Billy!

www. billyjonas.com

Graffiti People

These people need mustaches and funny glasses. Some may also need beards, tattoos, tacky hats, and more.

94

Madagascar Solitaire

The object of this game is to "jump" your game pieces until only one remains. It's harder than it looks!

SIMPLE VERSION

1 Place game pieces (coins, candy, potato chips) on every circle of the game board.

2 Remove one marker from the board. Eat it if it's food.

3 Take a game piece and jump over another one—landing in the one empty space.

4 Keep moving your pieces this way. You have to jump over a piece in order to move, and you can only jump over one piece at a time. You can move vertically or horizontally, but not diagonally.

5 If you end up with only one game piece on the board you win. If you have more than one and there are no moves left to make . . . not so much!

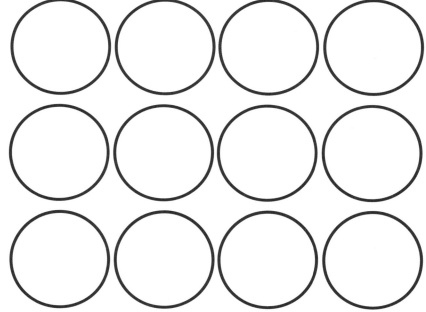

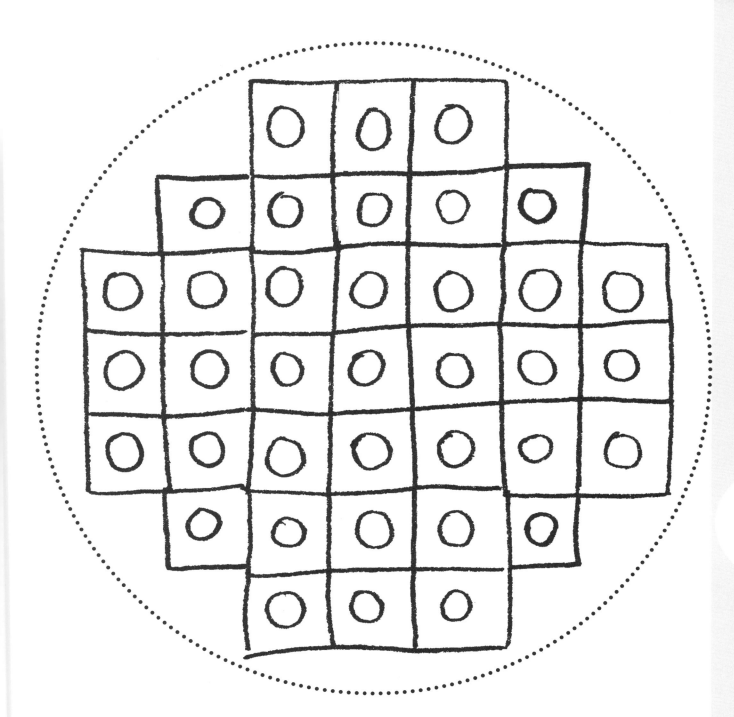

REALLY HARD VERSION

1 This is the real deal. You'll need 37 game pieces and a steady place to play. Your lap is not a steady place.

2 Remove the center game piece.

3 Move your pieces the same way you did in the simple version. Remember, no diagonal moves allowed.

A Different Sort of Alphabet

You've probably heard of codes where you replace shapes, dashes, or dots for letters. See if you can use the secret alphabet below to crack codes and write your own messages. Answers on page 252.

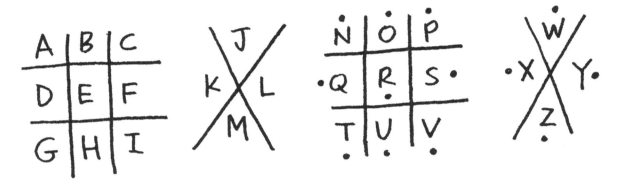

Write out the following in code:

Name: _____

Name of school: _____

Teacher's name: _____

Best friend: _____

Favorite vacation spot: _____

Sports you like: _____

Favorite book: _____

Favorite movie: _____

Now, make up your own for a friend to decipher.

_____

_____

_____

_____

_____

_____

_____

_____

Create-a-Cryptid

Cryptozoology is the study of legendary creatures that may or may not exist. Bigfoot, otherwise known as Sasquatch, Yeti, and Yowie, is the most famous of these well-known but rarely seen creatures.

The Loch Ness Monster is another cryptid that draws a lot of attention over in Scotland. Many cities and towns have stories about legendary creatures that lurk in the woods, lakes, ocean, etc. nearby. These stories are passed along through the years, along with reported sightings, some sort of evidence (a tuft of hair, a footprint, a photograph!), and more. Whether or not you believe in these creatures, it's a lot of fun to speculate about them. What's even more fun is to come up with your own! Follow the instructions below, and you'll have your own mysterious creature in no time.

Each cryptid needs a description. One of the best ways to start is to use an existing animal and add features that would make it seem otherworldly. (See the jackalope on the page 102 for an example.)

OFFICIAL NAME. You can use a long, complicated name that sounds Latin, if you wish.

_____

OTHER NAMES. Most cryptids have several names, suggesting that this creature has been around for some time.

_____

LOCATION. This is the area in which the cryptid has been sighted—otherwise known as its lurking grounds.

_____

HEIGHT or LENGTH, WEIGHT (if known).

_____

OTHER CHARACTERISTICS. Do you know what it eats, where it likes to live, whether it's nocturnal or not?

_____

EVIDENCE. Any footprints, hair or scales, bent twigs? Any of this can be used as evidence.

_____

_____

THE LEGEND. Include stories, sightings, and more.

_____

_____

_____

_____

_____

_____

_____

_____

_____

DRAW your cryptid here:

Gallery of Cryptids

Jackalope

Essentially a jackrabbit with antlers, this mythological creature has been known to roam the American West. It's extremely shy, but if found, can be milked— but only if it's asleep and on its belly. It's milk is reported to have medicinal qualities.

Current status among cryptozoologists: HOAX

The Jersey Devil

Reportedly sighted many times in New Jersey since the 1700s, this critter has been described as about four-feet tall with long neck, horse face, wings, and crane-like legs with hooves.

Current status among cryptozoologists: UNCONFIRMED

Mothman

In 1966-1967, more than 100 people in and around Point Pleasant, West Virginia reported seeing a seven-foot-tall, gray, man-like creature with large wings and red eyes. He chased a few people and caused a bit of a ruckus until he disappeared sometime in 1967. There's a twelve-foot statue of Mothman in Point Pleasant.

Current status among cryptozoologists: UNCONFIRMED

Manticore

The manticore appeared in ancient Persian and Greek folklore. This cryptid has the body of a red lion, a human head with three rows of teeth, and a voice that sounds like a trumpet.

Current status among cryptozoologists: MYTH/DISCREDITED

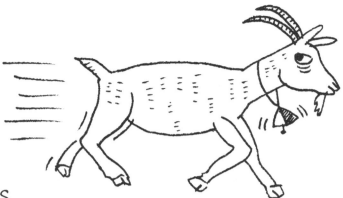

Chupacabras

This creature's name comes from two Spanish words that mean "to suck" and "goats." This is an appropriate name for this creature since it has been known to kill livestock by draining animals of their blood. (How nice!) First sighted in Puerto Rico, it has been described as a reptile or alien-like being with greenish-gray, leathery skin and spines running down its back. Some reports indicate it has wings, while others say it hops.

Current status among cryptozoologists: UNCONFIRMED

Loch Ness Monster

Known as "Nessie," and first sighted in Loch Ness in Scotland in the 600s, hundreds have since claimed to have seen this lake monster. Descriptions vary, but if you think of an Apatosaurus mixed with a dolphin, you'll get the drift.

Current status among cryptozoologists: UNCONFIRMED

Mongolian Death Worm

This guy is our favorite! Living in the Gobi Desert, this giant red worm (up to five feet long!) can supposedly spit sulfuric acid and electrocute you at the same time. Talk about overkill!

Current status among cryptozoologists: UNCONFIRMED

Giant Person-Eating Penguinocow

Sometimes glimpsed by children in speeding cars while on vacation, this seven-foot beast has a cow's head but a penguin's body. It hides among livestock at roadside pastures, and unlike real penguins, the Penguinocow can fly, reaching speeds of 55 mph. It has been known to chase vehicles with luggage bubbles on their roofs.

Current status among cryptozoologists: YOU'RE KIDDING, RIGHT!?

Crimez Aginst Grammer

While on the road, at an airport, or even just skimming a magazine, keep a sharp lookout for products and businesses that have forgotten how to spell and use punctuation.
We won't name any names here, but if these businesses were in our language arts classes, they would have failed!
Meanwhile, correct all the misspelled signs below!

PROOFREADER'S MARKS

If you want to cross out an incorrect word, do this: delete

If you want to capitalize a word, do this: capitalize

To add words or letters do this:

like
∧ cake.

(Corrections on page 252.)

Interview Your Parents

Sitting in a car, plane, train, or boat can be a good time to get to know your parents better. Use the questions below or come up with your own.

Good interviewers follow these tips: Don't ask simple yes/no questions. Don't interrupt—let them answer the question. Ask follow-up questions following your own curiosity. Get them when they're in the mood to talk. (Asking them questions when they're trying to find the right exit ramp is not a good idea.)

What's your earliest memory?

_____

_____

_____

Who was your best friend growing up? What did you do together?

_____

_____

_____

What kind of student were you?

_____

_____

Did you get into trouble a lot? Can you tell one memorable story about getting in trouble?

_____

_____

_____

Who was your favorite teacher? Why?

_____

_____

What were my grandparents like as parents?

_____

_____

_____

What did you like to do in your free time as a kid?

_____

_____

What kinds of pets did you have growing up?

_____

_____

What did you want to be when you were a kid?

_____

_____

Did you go to college? What was your major? Why did you pick that major?

_____

_____

What was your first job?

_____

_____

How did you get your first car?

_____

How did you meet mom/dad? Describe your first date.

_____

_____

_____

Would You Rather... Travel Edition

It's good to know your own mind. Which activities float your boat, and which don't?

Circle the activity you'd prefer. You have to choose one.

1. Wake up early so you can hike to the top of a mountain to watch the sun rise OR stay up late to look for shooting stars?

2. Sleep in a hotel OR sleep in a tent?

3. Travel by train OR by plane OR by car?

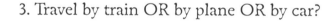

4. Eat something different and exotic every time you go to a restaurant OR eat something familiar and comforting?

5. Go to a foreign country for one week OR go on a beach vacation for a month?

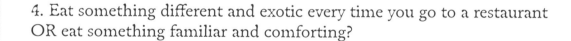

6. Have a surfboard on your car rack OR a snowboard?

7. Have a lazy, relaxing vacation with plenty of time to just "be" OR an action-packed, itinerary-filled vacation where you're on the go from morning till night?

8. Visit the world's best museums OR the world's most amazing natural wonders?

9. Visit a foreign country where you know the language OR a country where you don't know the language?

10. Explore the ocean's depths OR climb the highest peaks?

11. Take your best friend with you on a family vacation OR go on your best friend's family vacation?

Would You Rather...
the Miserable Travel Edition

Sometimes travel can be a challenge and not all trips end up being fun. Try not to unravel, and stay on the sunny side of the street.

Circle which you'd prefer.

1. Get a flat tire five miles from your vacation destination OR get a flat tire five miles from home after your vacation?

2. Have to go to the bathroom right after leaving a rest stop OR have to pull over because you're getting carsick?

3. Sit in the middle seat between two siblings (or friends) OR have a window seat but have the sun in your eyes the whole time?

4. Finally get to go on a plane trip but have to sit next to someone who snores OR sit next to someone who talks to you the entire trip?

5. Drink a flat cola that's cold OR drink a bubbly cola that's hot?

6. Have a rainy beach vacation OR a ski vacation with no snow?

7. Eat something at a restaurant you don't particularly like OR eat a favorite meal that ends up making you sick?

8. Work on your summer school assignment during a family trip OR leave it home and worry about it the whole time?

9. Find a strange insect in your hotel bed one morning OR have a hotel room with a mystery smell?

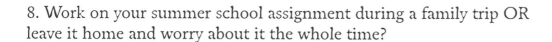

10. Have a four-hour family sing-along in the car OR listen to your least favorite song on an iPod for four hours?

11. Would you rather get poison ivy while camping OR go to the latrine and realize, just a little bit too late, that there's no toilet paper?

12. Get lost as a family OR know where you were but be by yourself?

13. Go to a foreign country where everyone seems to hate you OR stay home and have a bunch of hateful tourists visit your town?

14. Have the airline lose your luggage for a day OR miss your flight?

15. Catch a cold during your vacation

OR get stung by a bee?

If You Dare

What's the lowest amount of money you would accept to do the dares listed below? Read the dare, ponder your going price, and circle your going rate. If you'd never do it (no matter what!), circle "$10,000/never" and add the $10,000 to your total. When you're done, add up your earnings and check out your "risk factor."

Um . . . by the way, we're not encouraging you to actually do any of these dares; this is purely a speculative quiz!!!

We dare you to:

1. Eat a live slug.
$10 $50 $100 $1,000 $10,000/never

2. Walk barefoot on hot coals.
$10 $50 $100 $1,000 $10,000/never

3. Drink a smoothie with the following ingredients: bananas, strawberries, worms, ice cream, ice cubes, more worms.
$10 $50 $100 $1,000 $10,000/never

4. Stop turning in your homework for three weeks.
$10 $50 $100 $1,000 $10,000/never

5. Stop bathing for a month:
$10 $50 $100 $1,000 $10,000/never

6. Run at full speed into a solid wall.
$10 $50 $100 $1,000 $10,000/never

7. Get shot out of a circus cannon.
$10 $50 $100 $1,000 $10,000/never

8. Tightrope walk between two buildings (with net).
$10 $50 $100 $1,000 $10,000/never

9. Number 8 without a net.
$10 $50 $100 $1,000 $10,000/never

10. Dive off an Olympic diving board (the really high one).
$10 $50 $100 $1,000 $10,000/never

11. Spend the night in a graveyard with a friend.
$10 $50 $100 $1,000 $10,000/never

12. Number 11 . . . alone.
$10 $50 $100 $1,000 $10,000/never

13. Let someone drape 100 snakes on you.
$10 $50 $100 $1,000 $10,000/never

14. Same as #13, but with spiders.
$10 $50 $100 $1,000 $10,000/never

15. Ride your bike off a ramp into a lake.
$10 $50 $100 $1,000 $10,000/never

16. Kayak over a waterfall.
$10 $50 $100 $1,000 $10,000/never

17. Blast off into space.
$10 $50 $100 $1,000 $10,000/never

18. Skydive.
$10 $50 $100 $1,000 $10,000/never

19. Smell your dad's socks after a long day at work.
$10 $50 $100 $1,000 $10,000/never

20. Have your friends bury you up to your neck at the ocean's edge and leave you . . . as the tide's rising.
$10 $50 $100 $1,000 $10,000/never

Calculate your risk factor

Add up your dollar amount here:

$200-$2,000: You're a crazy, risk-taking adventurer, and we're sure your parents worry about you often.

$2,001-$20,000: You're pretty out-there adventurous, but you sometimes know the difference between risky and suicidal. Sometimes.

$20,001-$100,000: You have a healthy respect for potential danger.

$100,001-$200,000: You're a cautious, risk-adverse person. You're probably also extremely intelligent.

Recipes for the Road

Surprise your parents and show them what you can do in the kitchen! Whether camping out, going for a drive, flying half-way across the world, or simply vacationing at home, you need something good to eat. Here are some ideas that you can mix up yourself.

The–Whatever–You–Find–in–the–Kitchen–Cabinet Mix

In a large bowl, place a handful (or less) of nuts, dry cereal, raisins, seeds, dried fruits, pretzel pieces, sesame sticks, bite-size bagel chips, and anything else that might taste good thrown in. Once you have the right flavor, make enough for everyone and place in individual-sized, zip-lock plastic bags.

GORP (Good Ol' Raisins & Peanuts)

The name says it all, but the idea is that you can add to this simple masterpiece. After adding the same amount of peanuts and raisins, add some M&Ms, and a handful of sunflower seeds. And if the mixture isn't going to stay in the car for too long, you can also add some peanut butter chips. You can also try replacing the peanuts with almonds. Whatever you decide to add, make sure you have a good mix of crunchy, salty foods, and sweet, chewy items.

S'mores in a Bag

This one will make your stomach hurt. Mix up some mini-marshmallows, chocolate chips, and graham cracker pieces. Don't leave in the car for too long, and eat sparingly.

Baked Mix

Here's one you have to cook. Grab 1/2 cup of the following ingredients: dry-roasted nut mix, almonds, raisins, granola cereal, pumpkin seeds, and pretzel sticks. Toss them into a bowl and mix well. Add a 14-ounce can of sweetened condensed milk and mix again. Place in a greased baking pan and bake at 300°F for 30 minutes. Stir the mixture now and then while it's baking. Don't wait too long to eat this one, and don't leave it to bake in the car!

Fruit Salad

Only make this one if you'll have a cooler with you. Otherwise it won't keep for long. Chop up some of your favorite fruits: strawberries and other berries, bananas (may turn brown, but they still taste great!), melons, orange slices, apples, pears, pineapple, grapes, and perhaps some grapefruit if you like sour with your sweet. Mix the fruit in a bowl and keep it cold until you're ready to eat it. You can also add some nuts to the mix as well as shredded coconut.

Granola

Here's another baked treat that's great for a car ride or a hike. Place 3 cups of raw oats, 1 cup of shredded coconut, and 1-1/2 teaspoons of cinnamon in a baking dish. Mix well. In a bowl, add 1-1/2 cups of chopped nuts (whatever you like), 1/4 cup of honey, 1 teaspoon of vanilla extract, and 2 tablespoons of softened butter. Mix well and then pour this over the stuff in your baking dish. Mix it up and then bake at 325°F for 15 minutes or so.

Are We There Yet?
IN DIFFERENT LANGUAGES

If your parents are tired of hearing you ask, try asking in different languages.

SPANISH

"¿Ya llegamos?"

Už jsme tam?
CZECH

Burada henüz misiniz?

TURKISH

Có phải chúng ta có chưa?
VIETNAMESE

FRENCH

Er vi der endnu?
DANISH

Sind wir es noch?
GERMAN

Czy mamy tam jeszcze?
Polish

Ott vagyunk már?
HUNGARIAN

Are-ay e-way ere-thay et-yay?
PIG LATIN

Ubare wube thubere yubet?
UBBI DUBBI (another made up language in which "ub" is added before each vowel sound)

ITALIAN

The Ultimate Camping & Outdoor Adventure Quiz

Mother Nature can be a moody lady, so it's a good idea to have some basic knowledge about her before your set off into the wild blue yonder.

Answer the following true and false questions to see if you would survive an outdoor adventure! (Answers on page 253.)

1 While out hiking, try not to drink too much water.   TRUE   FALSE

2 If you're hungry, eat mushrooms along the trail.   TRUE   FALSE

3 When you retire for the evening, put your food up in a tree. TRUE   FALSE

4 If you must use the forest as a toilet, never do your duty within 200 feet of a water source.

TRUE   FALSE

5 Raccoons are friendly and like to be picked up and petted.

TRUE   FALSE

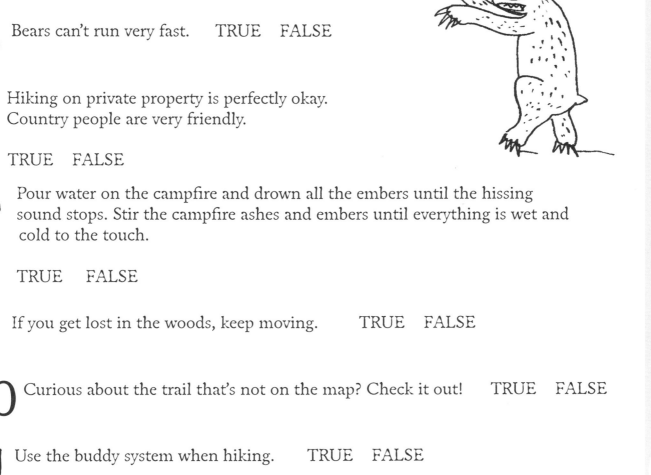

6 Bears can't run very fast.   TRUE   FALSE

7 Hiking on private property is perfectly okay. Country people are very friendly.

TRUE   FALSE

8 Pour water on the campfire and drown all the embers until the hissing sound stops. Stir the campfire ashes and embers until everything is wet and cold to the touch.

TRUE   FALSE

9 If you get lost in the woods, keep moving.   TRUE   FALSE

10 Curious about the trail that's not on the map? Check it out!   TRUE   FALSE

11 Use the buddy system when hiking.   TRUE   FALSE

12 Let people know where you'll be camping, and for how long.   TRUE   FALSE

13 Get a map and familiarize yourself with where you'll be hiking or camping.

TRUE   FALSE

14 Set up your tent next to the campfire.

TRUE   FALSE

15 If you get thirsty, drink water from streams and lakes.

TRUE   FALSE

16 Bathe in streams and lakes, and use lots of soap and shampoo.

TRUE   FALSE

17 Leaves of three, let them be.   TRUE   FALSE

18 Seek shelter under a tree or in a cave during a thunderstorm.   TRUE   FALSE

19 Invite the strange, long-haired dude who's talking to himself to dinner.   TRUE   FALSE

20 A long hike is a great time to break in those new hiking books.

TRUE   FALSE

SCORES

Scores below 10—
Survival is doubtful!

Scores above 11-15—
You have a fighting chance!

16 and above—
You're an ultimate survivor.

BRAVO!

Fun Things to Do with Your Digital Camera

Shoot Your Teddy Bear . . .

. . . with your camera, of course! When traveling and vacationing, take along a favorite stuffed animal or doll. Take pictures of all the sights with your friend in the photos. Then email the photos to friends along with written accounts of your friend's adventures.

The Close-up Game

This game is particularly fun to play when trapped in an airplane or car or while taking a nature hike. One person takes a photo of an item from up close, while the other players aren't looking. The other players then have to guess what the item is. Take turns, and save the pictures for friends when you return home.

The Great Alphabet Hunt

Find the alphabet in nature. While hiking or camping, take pictures of anything in nature that looks like one of the letters of the alphabet. You can't use signs, and try to do this without moving anything. See if you can collect all 26! Try this in an urban setting, too.

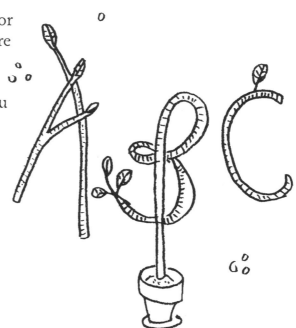

X-Ray Screening Fun

Airport security is serious business. That doesn't mean you can't have fun imagining what the screeners will find in these suitcases and bags.

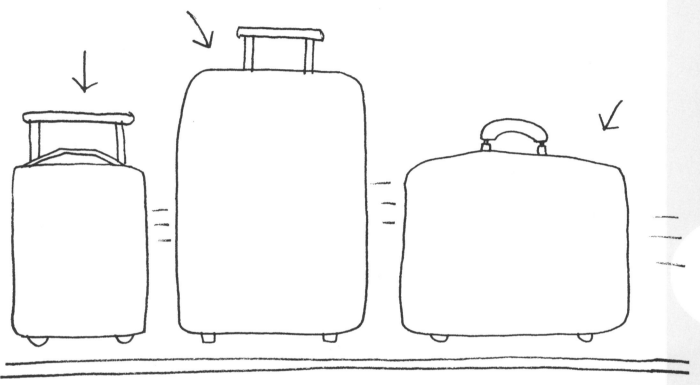

Down the Road

Did you know you could predict your future while on the road? Follow the directions below and you'll know all about yourself and the rest of your family and friends.

1 Multiply the day of your birth by 3. So if you were born on May 16, multiply 16 by 3, which equals 48. Write your birth day x 3 here:

_____

2 Use the number you came up with and count out that many cars, trucks, motorcycles, etc. that *pass your car*.

What kind of vehicle is it?: _____
This is the type of vehicle you will drive.

What is the license plate number of that vehicle?: _____

3 Write down the first two numbers in the license plate. (So, if the license plate of your car of the future is XXY-2458, your number is 24.)

First two numbers: _____

4 Count as many cars *that you pass* as the number you wrote down in #3. Write down that car's license plate: _____

5 Write down the numbers in the license plate and add 3 zeroes to the end of it. So, if the license plate is W3B-99X, the number you'd write down would be 399,000. This will be your yearly salary! If the license plate has no numbers, you will be in the poorhouse. If the license plate is a vanity plate, you'll be a billionaire.

6 Now take the first two numbers in the license plate you wrote down in #4, and add them together. If there were no numbers, take the first two letters, figure out what number they are in the alphabet and add them—use this number for step 7.

7 Count that many cars, trucks, etc. that *pass you*. Then count the number of people in the vehicle. This is how many children you will have.

Write down the license plate of this vehicle: _____

8 Take the first number in this license plate (or letter like in step 6) and count that many exits you pass. Write down the exit number you land on:_____

9 Now, count that many business names you pass. These could be buildings, signs, trucks. The one you land on is where you will work.

10 Write down the next exit number you see: _____.

11 Count that many houses you pass on the road. The one you land on is the kind you'll live in. Don't forget to count apartment buildings, trailers, RVs, etc.

12 Look at your car's odometer. Take the last two numbers and count out that many out-of-state license plates. The one you land on is where you will live.

Easy Peasy Car Games

These games are fun, easy to play, and may last five seconds, five minutes, or even five hours. Thanks to Maggie and Erin for giving us the first two!

Wee & Woo

When the car veers left, making you lean to the right, say, "Weeeee." When the car veers right, making you lean to the left, say, "Woooo." Exaggerate your leaning for extra fun. That's it. This is a good game to play with a little brother or sister.

Gain a Window, Lose a Window

Two people can play this game, and they need to be looking out windows on opposite sides of the car. It helps if mom or dad drives in the middle lane. You each start with six windows. If you see a white car, you lose a window. If you see a green car, you get a window. Whoever runs out of windows first, loses. Try this with different colored or types of vehicles.

Stump the Parents

Kids in the back seat yell out a first name. The parents have to come up with at least two famous people with that first name (movie star, author, character from a book, athlete). If they do, they get a point. If they don't, the kids get a point. First team to 20 points wins.

Yes/No, You're Out!

Ask a person in the car a series of questions about themselves. They can answer in any way, except they can't answer with a "Yes" or "No." They can't stop to think about it, they have to answer the questions honestly, and they can't answer the same way twice. If they do any of the above, it's the other person's time to be questioned.

License Plate Hunt

Use this map to mark off all the state license plates you find.
We left the state names off this map for extra fun.

Draw These Roads

People who give names to streets and roads can be wildly creative or ponderously predictable. Illustrate the roads listed here. Let the names direct your drawings.

Lonesome Highway

Spaghetti Junction

Future Lane (Dead End)

English Ivy Turnpike

Candy Cane Lane

Rocky Road

You're So Punny!

A PUN is the funny use of a word or words, which are formed or sound alike but have different meanings—literally, a play on words. They are a very old form of humor, but new puns are still being invented. Feel free to come up with your own. Expect a few groans though.

Illustrate the following puns.

EXAMPLE:

groan . . .

"Lawn mooer"

Did you hear about the guy whose whole left side was cut off? He's all right now.

Poultry in Motion

Acupuncture Is a Jab Well Done

Propaganda:
A Gentlemanly Goose

A very small alien says, "Take me to your ladder."

Time Traveler's Checks

Sometimes it's fun to travel into the future to see what your life will look like. What will you be wearing, doing, eating, playing, and paying for?

Well, what if we gave you $100,000 to spend anyway you like? We can't REALLY do that, but we can give you 100,000 "future dollars," which you can spend as you see fit.

Fill out the transaction register book on the next page with your future purchases, and see how much you think it will all cost.

USED CAR LOT OF THE FUTURE

Transaction Register

DATE	PAYEE	TRANSACTION DESCRIPTION	AMOUNT	BALANCE
Remember, it's the future	This is a fancy way of saying, "the person you are paying"	Briefly describe the cool futuristic thing you are buying here	List the cost of your purchase	How much money you're starting with
				$100,000

Start subtracting from this amount

133

Halfway There

Here are some half-drawn pictures. Finish them up for us.

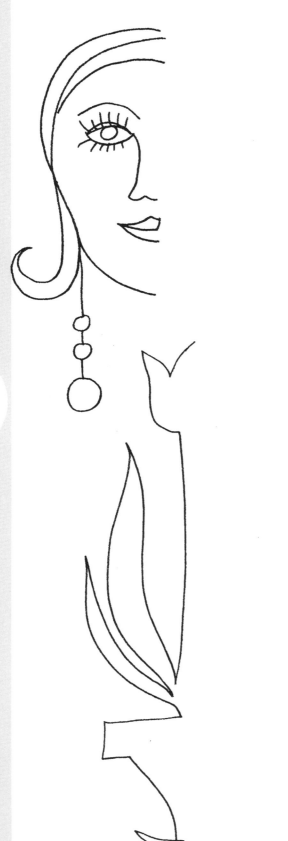

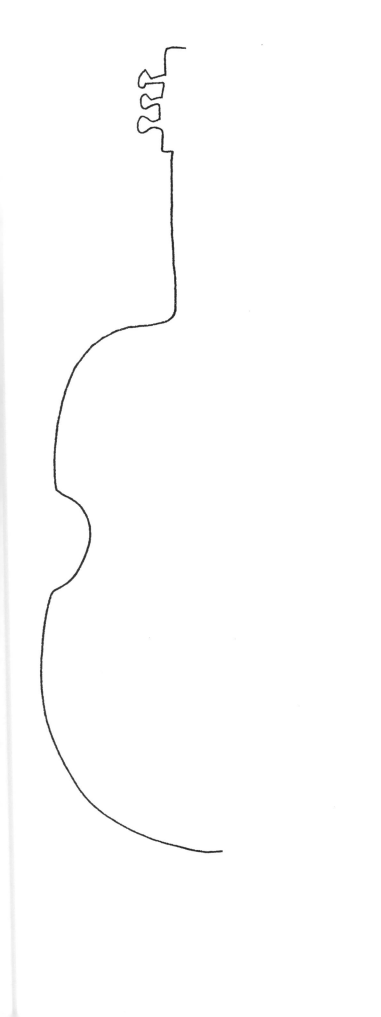

If...

Ask yourself and your traveling companions
the following questions.

1. If you were an animal, what would you be?

_____

2. If you were a mood, what would you be?

_____

3. If you were dessert, what would you be?

_____

4. If you were a can of beans, what would you be?

_____

5. If you were an ice cream flavor, what flavor would you be?

_____

6. If you were a musical instrument, which would you be?

_____

7. If you were a cartoon character, who would you be?

_____

8. If you were an electric device, what would you be?

_____

9. If you were a character from a book, who would you be?

_____

10. If you were a car, what kind of car would you be?

_____

11. If you were a musician, what type of music would you play?

_____

12. If you were an insect, what would you be?

_____

13. If you were a scientist, what kind would you be?

_____

14. If you were a teacher, what would you teach?

_____

15. If you were a wizard (or a witch), who would you be?

_____

16. If you were a piece of mail, what kind of mail would you be?

_____

17. If you were a road, what kind would you be?

_____

18. If you were a book, what would you be?

_____

19. If you were a plant, what would you be?

_____

20. If you can be anything, what will you be?

_____

Go a
Little Nuts

Draw as many squirrels as you can on
the next two pages. Don't forget the acorns!

Follow these 4 simple steps and you'll have yourself a squirrel!

THESE ARE A FEW OF MY
favorite things

Listing what you LOVE and sharing that with others
is a good way to get to know people. Feel free to doodle
some of these things too.

Animals

_____

_____

Friends

_____

_____

_____

Teachers

_____

_____

School subjects

_____

_____

Movies

_____

_____

Books

_____

_____

_____

Toys

_____

_____

Commercials

_____

_____

TV shows

_____

_____

_____

Family moments

_____

_____

Memories

_____

_____

Sports

_____

_____

Games

_____

_____

Pets

_____

_____

Clothing

_____

_____

Chores

_____

Stores

_____

_____

Things with wheels

_____

_____

Websites

_____

_____

Things in your room

_____

_____

Words

_____

_____

Sayings

_____

_____

Food

_____

Vacations

_____

_____

THESE ARE A FEW OF MY
least favorite things

Listing what you CAN'T STAND and sharing that with others is also a good way to get to know people. Feel free to doodle some of these things, too.

142

Animals

_____

_____

Friends

_____

_____

_____

Teachers

_____

_____

School subjects

_____

_____

Movies

_____

_____

Books

_____

_____

_____

Toys

_____

_____

Commercials

_____

_____

TV shows

_____

_____

Family moments

_____

Memories

_____

Sports

_____

Games

_____

Pets

_____

Clothing

_____

Chores

_____

Stores

_____

Things with wheels

_____

Websites

_____

Things in your room

_____

Words

_____

Sayings

_____

Foods

_____

Vacations

_____

143

Tahk Like a Movie Stahr!

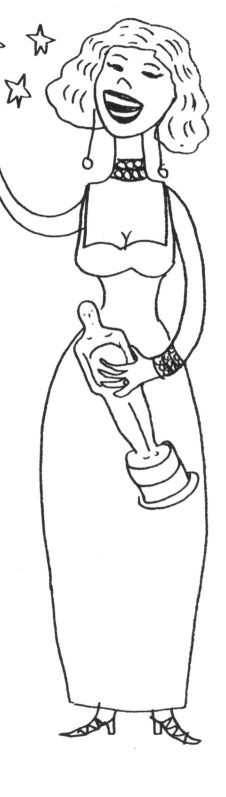

Ever get tired of being yourself? Tired of your neighbor being him/herself? Try this exercise.

Pick three numbers out of a hat (or have someone choose three numbers from 1 to 10 for you). The first number is who you will be in Column A. The second number is who your friend will become in Column B. The third number is what you will talk about for at least five minutes (Column C).

Have fun, dahlings.

144

	A	B	C
1	Ninety-year old	Paranoid person	Sports
2	Teenager	Movie star	Weather
3	Rocket scientist	Two-year old	Politics
4	Shy salesperson	Robot	School
5	Opera singer	Bully	This book
6	Movie preview announcer	Politician	Celebrities
7	Romanian vampire	Principal	Favorite books
8	Cheerleader	Spy	Movies
9	Beach bum	TV game-show host	Clothing & shoes
10	Gym teacher	Cave person	BFFs

Useful Road Signs

The following traffic laws and warnings need signs just as much as STOP and YIELD do. And you're just the person for the job.

- Alien crossing
- No yelling zone
- Drive on any side of the road you want
- No speed limit
- Littering is punishable by death
- Waving to other cars is not allowed
- Dirty gas station bathrooms ahead
- Road work ahead. But nobody's really doing anything.
- If you're on this road, you're lost
- Right here: 0 miles

Total *Remote* Control

This is no ordinary remote control. With it you can control anything you want. Sister annoying you? The "Power" button can silence her for up to two hours! You get to decide what each button's purpose is. Will these buttons be for good (press "2" for world peace) or for evil (press fast forward button and money will fall out of parking meters)? Your choice.

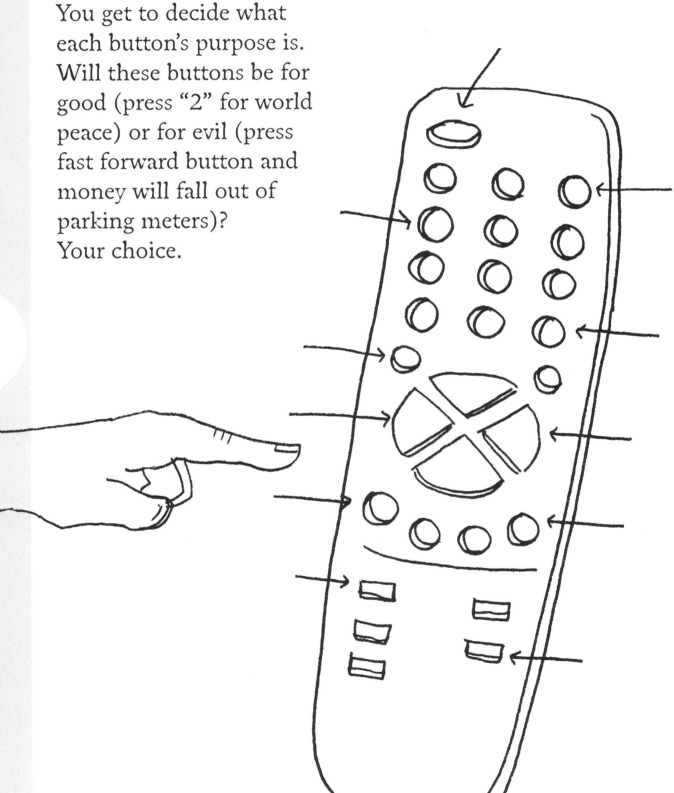

Shrine to Unforgettable Days

Devote this pages to the collected memories of your vacation. Tape or glue ticket stubs, pieces of maps, fortunes from fortune cookies or whatever you have collected to the shrine below. Write down snippets of your favorite moments and draw in a picture from your trip in the main box.

Cut this page out of the book and save it in a scrapbook if you wish. Don't forget to date it.

Overheard

Take this book with you on your next walk. Listen carefully and write down any overheard dialog you come across. Try not to be obvious about it. It's no fun getting caught. See if you can come up with a story using your found words. Maybe you have a future as a detective or a journalist.

Eavesdropping . . .

. . . means to listen secretly to a private conversation. The word "eaves" refers to the edge of a roof that overhangs the side of a building. A person who stood at the eavesdrop of a house to listen to what was happening inside would be called an "eavesdropper." It's an old English word for busybody, sleuth, or snooper. Call it what you like, just don't get caught.

151

Create a Hero

Most superheroes aren't born super. Some unfortunate accident makes them that way. Spider Man got bit by a spider, the Hulk was exposed to gamma rays . . . you get the idea. Name and draw the superheroes who are created by the following incidents.

DANG!

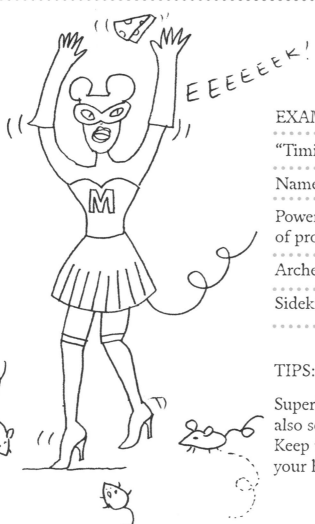

EEEEEEK!

EXAMPLE:

"Timid teenager is harassed by 3 blind mice."

Name: MOUSE GIRL!!!

Powers: Able to eat large quantities of processed cheese food in a single sitting.

Archenemy: Cat Woman

Sidekick: Rat Boy

TIPS:

Superheroes often have really big muscles. They also seem to wear a lot of capes and jumpsuits. Keep these things in mind when you're drawing your heroes.

"Mild-mannered man falls into vat of mystery meat at fast-food processing plant."

Name:

Powers:

Archenemy:

Sidekick:

"Boy spends 89 hours straight playing Guitar Hero."

Name:

Powers:

Archenemy:

Sidekick:

Create a Hero

"During a disastrous human triangle a cheerleader ingests two whole metallic pom poms."

Name:

Powers:

Archenemy:

Sidekick:

"Girl gets bitten by her annoying, radioactive little brother."

Name:

Powers:

Archenemy:

Sidekick:

"Boy sees uneaten donut in a street-corner garbage can. Decides to eat it."

Name:

Powers:

Archenemy:

Sidekick:

NOW, MAKE UP YOUR OWN!

Name:

Powers:

Archenemy:

Sidekick:

Please Sign on the Dotted Line

Many people collect signatures of famous people. On this page, collect the signatures of interesting people you meet in your travels (even if they aren't famous . . . yet). You may have to ask a question or two in order to find out if they fit any of the descriptions below.

1. Has travelled more than 500 miles to be where you are right now

....

2. Has a tattoo

....

3. Has been married for 25 years or longer

....

4. Is a vegetarian

....

5. Rides a motorcycle

....

6. Is in the Armed Forces

....

7. Collects something interesting

....

8. Likes licorice

....

9. Is a farmer

....

10. Can juggle

....

11. Can touch his nose with his tongue

....

12. Wears a hat

....

13. Wears lots of jewelry

....

14. Likes to sing

....

15. Plays a musical instrument

....

16. Has met someone famous

....

17. Has jumped out of an airplane

....

18. Is or was a teacher

....

19. Has more than one pet

....

20. Seems really happy

....

Suited to a T

Think about all the people in your life and how happy they would be if you gave them personalized T-shirts made by you!

Maybe mom would like a "Punk Rock Rules!" shirt with well-placed rips. Maybe your brother would like a hemp shirt with a "Save the Earth" logo on it printed with vegetable-based inks. Here's your design studio. Create away! Feel free to draw in the heads and arms, if you like.

Your Pet's Diary

At some point during your trip, you're going to start missing all the things you left behind: your stuff, your friends, and especially your pet or pets. You might even be worried about your dog, cat, guinea pig, or snake. How is she getting along without you? Is she miserable or having the time of her life?

For Example:

Dear Diary,

Friday evening I was missing my human so much, I threw caution to the wind and invited that cute cockatiel from down the street over for dinner . . .

Imagine your pet decided to write a diary of her time while you're away. Give her a great time with lots of parties and adventures.

Dear Diary,

....

....

....

....

....

....

160

I ♥ MY SNAKE!

Your Pet's Biography

If you're still missing your favorite nonhuman friend, write your pet's biography here. Start with his birth (if you know it), and then write about when you adopted each other. Write about what your pet does during the day when you're at school. Ask your family for help with the details.

Biography of:

....

....

....

....

....

....

....

....

....

....

....

....

....

Draw a picture of
your beloved beasty

163

Tic-Tac-Dough

This game is just like the regular tic-tac-toe, except you use money instead of Xs and Os.

One player is evens and the other is odds. You take turns placing one of your numbers in an empty square. (You can only use each number once.) The object is to be the first person to get a horizontal, vertical, or diagonal row that adds up to $15. It doesn't matter if the numbers in the row are all even or odd, just that they add up to $15.

164

SAMPLE GAME:

1st player's turn
$2, $4, $6, $8, $10
$1, $3, $5, $7, $9

2nd player's turn
$2, $4, $6, $8, $10
$1, $3, $5, $7, $9

1st player's turn
$2, $4, $6, $8, $10
$1, $3, $5, $7, $9

2nd player's turn
$2, $4, $6, $8, $10
$1, $3, $5, $7, $9

1st player's turn
$2, $4, $6, $8, $10
$1, $3, $5, $7, $9

Player 2 wins!
$2, $4, $6, $8, $10
$1, $3, $5, $7, $9

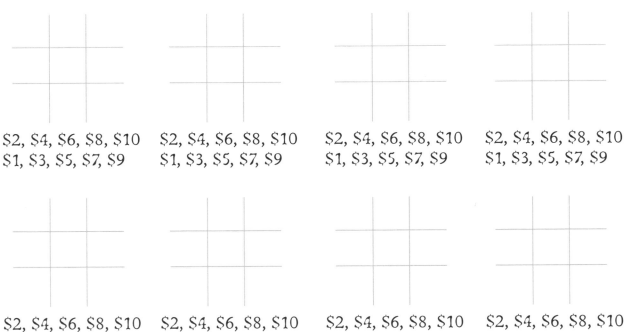

$2, $4, $6, $8, $10
$1, $3, $5, $7, $9

$2, $4, $6, $8, $10
$1, $3, $5, $7, $9

$2, $4, $6, $8, $10
$1, $3, $5, $7, $9

$2, $4, $6, $8, $10
$1, $3, $5, $7, $9

$2, $4, $6, $8, $10
$1, $3, $5, $7, $9

$2, $4, $6, $8, $10
$1, $3, $5, $7, $9

$2, $4, $6, $8, $10
$1, $3, $5, $7, $9

$2, $4, $6, $8, $10
$1, $3, $5, $7, $9

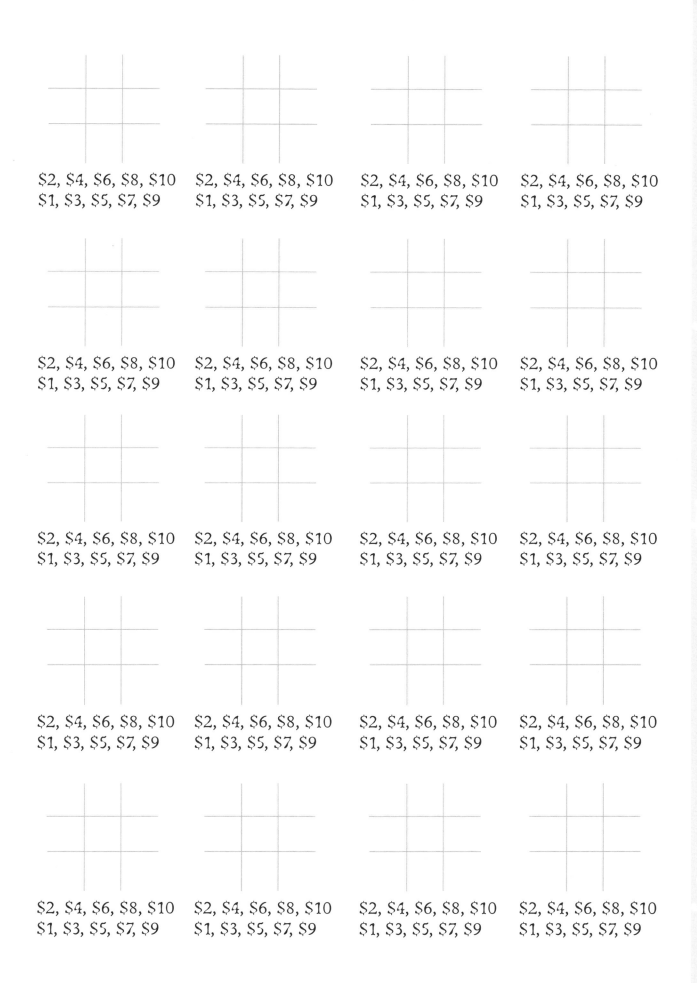

$2, $4, $6, $8, $10
$1, $3, $5, $7, $9

$2, $4, $6, $8, $10
$1, $3, $5, $7, $9

$2, $4, $6, $8, $10
$1, $3, $5, $7, $9

$2, $4, $6, $8, $10
$1, $3, $5, $7, $9

$2, $4, $6, $8, $10
$1, $3, $5, $7, $9

$2, $4, $6, $8, $10
$1, $3, $5, $7, $9

$2, $4, $6, $8, $10
$1, $3, $5, $7, $9

$2, $4, $6, $8, $10
$1, $3, $5, $7, $9

$2, $4, $6, $8, $10
$1, $3, $5, $7, $9

$2, $4, $6, $8, $10
$1, $3, $5, $7, $9

$2, $4, $6, $8, $10
$1, $3, $5, $7, $9

$2, $4, $6, $8, $10
$1, $3, $5, $7, $9

$2, $4, $6, $8, $10
$1, $3, $5, $7, $9

$2, $4, $6, $8, $10
$1, $3, $5, $7, $9

$2, $4, $6, $8, $10
$1, $3, $5, $7, $9

$2, $4, $6, $8, $10
$1, $3, $5, $7, $9

$2, $4, $6, $8, $10
$1, $3, $5, $7, $9

$2, $4, $6, $8, $10
$1, $3, $5, $7, $9

$2, $4, $6, $8, $10
$1, $3, $5, $7, $9

$2, $4, $6, $8, $10
$1, $3, $5, $7, $9

Diary of a Madman (or Woman!)

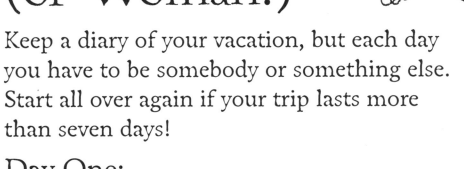

Keep a diary of your vacation, but each day you have to be somebody or something else. Start all over again if your trip lasts more than seven days!

Day One:

(From the point of view of one of your parents.)

_____

_____

_____

_____

Day Two:

(From the point of view of a sibling.)

_____

_____

_____

_____

Day Three:

(As if you woke up this morning beamed into this family and this trip for the first time. You have no idea who these people are or where you even are.)

_____

_____

_____

_____

Day Four:

(Today's even worse. You're an alien.)

_____

_____

_____

_____

Day Five:

(From the point of view of your suitcase.)

_____

_____

_____

_____

Day Six:

(From the point of view of the car you're driving around in.)

_____

_____

_____

_____

Day Seven:

(From the point of view of the main attraction you saw or experienced today—ocean, statue, museum, hiking trail . . .)

_____

_____

_____

_____

It's Raining Frogs

Make it rain frogs on these poor people.

No Joke!

Raining frogs is a rare meteorological phenomenon. This crazy occurrence has been documented all over the world. Scientists believe this may happen when a tornado (water spout) travels over water and sweeps the animals up into the air and drops them like rain. It has also been known to rain fish and birds.

Long & Winding Road GAMES

Instead of whining, eating junk food, or begging
for yet another bathroom break, try these games.

Unintended Acronyms

Read off the letters of a passing car's license plate. Everybody in the car has to think of a phrase that starts with those letters. So, if the license plate is WEA-946, the letters are WEA, and some of the phrases could be, "Weird English Antelopes," "We Eat Asparagus," "Women Equally Angry." The group then votes which one was the most awesome. (You can't vote for your own.) The person with the most votes gets a point. First person to 10 points wins.

Trunk Memory Game

Have each traveling companion (except the driver) stand in front of the car's full trunk before leaving or during a rest break. Try to memorize everything that's in the trunk and where it's located. Once you're on the road, draw what you remember. At the next stop, compare drawings to the trunk and see who came the closest.

Find the Alphabet

Look for letters in the alphabet in order. Use only signs you see along the road. License plates don't count.

Who Can Be the Most Quiet

First person who makes a sound loses. Your parents will, for some reason, love this game.

Sweet and Sour

Wave and smile at the people in cars passing you. If the people smile and wave back, they are SWEET. If they ignore you or are rude in response to your greetings, they are SOUR. Keep track of how many SWEETS and SOURS you come across in a 20-mile portion of your trip. Good luck, and try to stay sweet yourself.

Worth Mentioning

Write down the most interesting names of towns, cities, restaurants, people, and road names you come across. Use them in a story or a poem.

EXAMPLE:

"*Spunky Puddle, Ohio* was an interesting place. We ate the "*CheesyMeatyMan*" lunch special at a diner called, *The Baggy Goose*. Unfortunately, Mom started to feel sick by the time we reached *Butzville, New Jersey*."

_____

_____

_____

_____

_____

_____

Not Worth Mentioning, and Yet . . .

Write down the dullest names of towns, cities, restaurants, people, and road names you come across. Use them in a story or a poem.

_____

_____

_____

_____

_____

_____

Making Tracks

What keeps you from falling flat
on your face? The answer may be
on the bottom of your shoes.

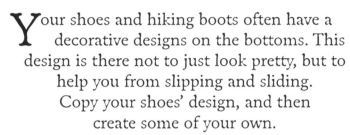

Your shoes and hiking boots often have a decorative designs on the bottoms. This design is there not to just look pretty, but to help you from slipping and sliding. Copy your shoes' design, and then create some of your own.

172

COUNTRIES
You've Never Heard Of
(Unless You Live There)

Never Heard of it!

Tuvalu

Is a Polynesian island (actually four reef islands and five atolls) located in the Pacific Ocean between Hawaii and Australia—making it one of the most remote countries in the world. There are only 12,000 people on the island, and it's only around 10 square miles. Your hometown is probably bigger. Much bigger.

Bhutan

Because of its violent storms, Bhutan is known by its inhabitants as *Druk Yul*, which means "land of the thunder dragon." This country is a remote, mountainous, landlocked nation in South Asia that's bordered by India and China. Known as one of the most isolated nations in the world, tourists have only been able to visit since 1974. The population stands at 2 million, with Buddhism being the primary religion. Bhutan prides itself in its ability to protect their natural resources and their traditional culture.

Andorra

Few textbooks mention Andorra when discussing Europe. Located in the eastern Pyrenees mountain range and sort of squashed between France and Spain, this small country's population (84,000 people) can all fit in a large football stadium. Andorra is generally prosperous due to its tourism industry, with the number of annual tourists numbering more than 100-times the population. People flock to the area for the resorts as well as the fact that they don't have to pay taxes!

Andorra Tidbits
• There are no airports, railroads, or ports in Andorra.
• The native Andorrans are outnumbered by European immigrants.

Bhutan Tidbits
• Their national sport is archery.
• The country was rated "happiest in Asia" in a recent poll.
• Their government operates under the philosophy known as GROSS NATIONAL HAPPINESS, in which modernization and economic wellness are balanced by spiritual, mental, and physical wellness in order to maintain a high quality of life.

Tuvalu Tidbits
• Tuvalu is the fourth smallest country—it's only about 1/10th the size of Washington DC. Only Vatican City (yes, it's a country!), Monaco, and Nauru are smaller.
• There is no fresh water or much farmable land, so fish and coconuts are the only local foods available. They import most of their food and catch rainwater to drink. They also have a desalinization plant that turns salt water from the ocean into drinkable water.
• The country makes money by leasing their internet domain name, tv; selling stamps and coins to collectors; and tourism.

N
W   E
S

Suriname Tidbits

• Its official language is Dutch, and it only gained its independence from the Netherlands in 1975.
• The English ruled Suriname but traded it to the Dutch in 1667 for New Amsterdam, which later became New York.
• Many of the Netherlands' best soccer players are of Surinamese descent.

Eritrea Tidbits

• One of the oldest hominid fossils (possible missing link between apes and humans) was found in Eritrea in 1995. The skull was found to be more than 1 million years old. Archeologists have also discovered some of the earliest remains of human tools here.
• Cycling is one of Eritrea's favorite sports, and there's even a Tour of Eritrea held every year, which is a 10-day, 700 mile race that travels through desert lowlands, dangerous mountainous climbs, and windy coastline.

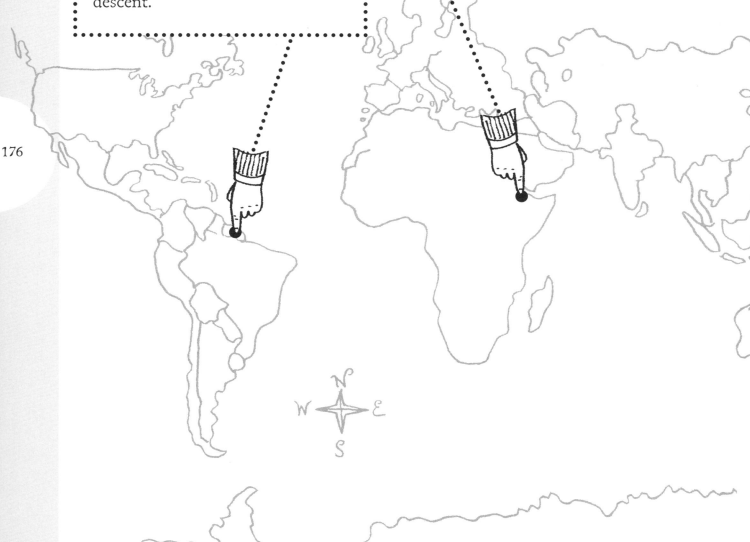

Suriname

At nearly 1 million square miles, Suriname is the smallest country on the South American continent. Most of its 430,000 people live near the coast since 80% of its land is nearly uninhabitable due to tropical rainforest. Mining is its biggest industry (alumina, gold, crude oil).

Eritrea

Eritrea, a former Italian colony, is a country in northeastern Africa, located in what's known as the Horn of Africa. Its border along the Red Sea has made it a strategic location for shipping and commerce; however, due to political problems, wars, and drought, most of its population lives in poverty.

Make Up Your Own Tiny Country

Name of Country:

_____

Where Is It?

_____

Population:

_____

Official Language:

_____

Unusual Customs:

_____

Main Export:

_____

Tourist Attractions:

_____

What a Sty!

How many pigs can fit onto the next two pages?
Don't forget the piglets.

Follow these 4 simple steps and oink, oink!

Poems for the Road

You might think a long trip a tad tedious after a while, but what if you took the common sights, sounds, and even smells of your trip and wrote poems about them?

FOR EXAMPLE, you're tired of seeing road kill. It bothers you. Write an epitaph or elegy, which is a thoughtful poem about someone who has died.

To the poor dead groundhog we just whizzed by,

who loved his territory along the side of the road

until stricken by the need

to see what was on the other side.

Okay, perhaps that wasn't very thoughtful, but we think you'll get our meaning. Match up the possible themes with a different kind of poem and give it a try. Or, just start writing!

Topics

- The slow car ahead of you

- The mystery smell in the car

- Gas station attendants

- Billboards

- Squashed sandwiches in the cooler

- Big rigs

- What your parents are talking about in the front seat

- Something you forgot at home

- Your seat

- Siblings

- Fast-food restaurants

- Come up with your own!

Types of Poems

ACROSTIC: A poem in which certain letters, usually the first in each line, form a word or message.

BALLAD: Tells a story that's meant to be a folktale or legend.

BURLESQUE: Treats a serious subject in a funny way.

EPIC: Tells of a heroic figure. Usually long.

EPITAPH: An inscription on a tombstone written to praise the deceased.

HAIKU: Composed of three unrhymed lines of five, seven, and five syllables.

LIMERICK: Consists of five lines in which lines 1, 2, and 5 rhyme and 3 and 4 rhyme. See example below for a sense of the rhythm.

LIST POEM: Made up of a list of items or events.

LYRIC: Expresses the thoughts and feelings of the poet.

NARRATIVE: Tells a story.

ODE: A celebration of an object.

SHAPE POEM: Written in the shape an object.

WRITE YOUR POEMS HERE

Travel Limerick

There once was a family named Cotton,
Who when traveling together got rotten,
They pinched, kicked, and fought,
And arrived quite distraught,
But two minutes later: all forgotten!

Round and Round

What can you doodle using only circles and ellipses?
Look all around you for inspiration.

183

What Are These People Boycotting?

You decide. It could be many different things or one big thing.

Montgomery Bus Boycott

The Montgomery Bus Boycott was a year-long protest in Montgomery, Alabama, which galvanized the American Civil Rights Movement and led to a 1956 decision by the U.S. Supreme Court declaring segregated seating on buses unconstitutional. This all started because a brave activist named Rosa Parks, who refused to sit at the back of the bus.

I'll Have the Sheep Stomach with a Side Order of Dead Bugs

When visiting exotic locales, you may run into some foods that are outside your comfort zone. What do we mean? Well, perhaps the meat in your sandwich has eyes or the crunchy snack you're enjoying is really fried grasshoppers!

Our advice? Well, first off, remember that certain foods that we classify as strange are yummy delicacies for others. Next, live in the moment and take a bite! The people you're visiting will admire your courage, and you might feel more at home even if you're thousands of miles away. We have scoured the world looking for the most exotic and unusual foods. Would you try them?

Haggis

Originating in Scotland, this tasty meal features minced sheep liver, heart, and lung, mixed with spices, oatmeal, and more. Oh yeah, these ingredients are then boiled in the sheep's stomach for hours. According to some, haggis looks and tastes like cooked ground beef, while others describe the taste as nutty and savory. It's traditionally served with neeps and tatties, which are turnips and potatoes.

WOULD YOU EAT IT?
YES, PLEASE   NO, THANK YOU

Casu Marzu

This sheep milk cheese is made on the island of Sardinia, which is off the coast of Italy. Its name means "rotten cheese," mostly because it has maggots crawling inside it. The larvae are put in the cheese on purpose in order to help the fermentation process. The cheese should only be eaten while the maggots are still alive. If not, the cheese is toxic. But be careful. Before taking a bite of casu marzu, cover your eyes, because the maggots can jump up to six inches and may decide to take a leap into your eye. Those who have tried it say it burns your mouth, smells like old smelly socks, and tastes rotten. Unfortunately, this cheese is now illegal, so you'll have a hard time finding it. Plus, those pesky maggots are bad for your stomach.

WOULD YOU EAT IT?   YES, PLEASE   NO, THANK YOU

Beondegi

This is one of South Korea's most popular snack-food items. You can buy them from street vendors nearly everywhere you go. What is beondegi? It's boiled, steamed, or deep-fried silkworm pupae. It's said to have either a nutty taste or a flavor similar to crab meat.

WOULD YOU EAT IT?   YES, PLEASE   NO, THANK YOU

Chapulines

If you happen to visit the Mexican cities of Oaxaca or Puebla, you're sure to run into chapulines, which are eaten like nuts, popcorn, or potato chips. And once you get over the fact that chapulines are cooked and seasoned grasshoppers, you'll be popping them in your mouth, much like the locals have been doing for more than 3,000 years. This crunchy snack is usually seasoned with lime or chili, and you can eat them right out of the bag or put them in your taco or sandwich.

WOULD YOU EAT IT?
YES, PLEASE   NO, THANK YOU

Fugu

Fugu is a Japanese dish made from the meat of a puffer fish, which contains lethal amounts of poison. Only licensed and trained chefs are allowed to prepare it, but people still die from eating this sometimes. When eating it, you may feel a small prickling sensation, which is caused by the small amounts of poison in the meat.

WOULD YOU EAT IT?   YES, PLEASE   NO, THANK YOU

Bird Nest Soup

It's probably not difficult to determine what's in this Chinese soup, is it!? This soup is made from the nests of swiftlets, which are tiny birds that live in caves. Swiftlets don't use twigs and leaves to build their nests, they use their own saliva (spit), which hardens into a gummy like substance when exposed to air. The soup has a rubbery texture and tastes like … soup! These nests are not easily obtained, which is why this dish is known as the "Caviar of the East."

WOULD YOU EAT IT?   YES, PLEASE   NO, THANK YOU

Grandma's Gelatin Salad

Gelatin (from French *gélatine*) is a translucent, colorless, odorless, brittle, nearly tasteless solid substance derived from the collagen inside animals' skin and bones. It's used as a binding agent in many foods, and when combined with sweeteners, fruit flavors, and bright colors—to make desserts. Special molded pans are designed to hold these gelatin mixtures and give them unique shapes.

Gelatin salads have been known to include berry, lemon, and lime flavors, with shredded cabbage, marshmallows, cottage cheese, pineapple pieces, minced nuts, sliced cucumbers, and ground horseradish thrown in. This truly is a wiggly and weird food.

WOULD YOU EAT IT?   YES, PLEASE   NO, THANK YOU

Here are some other delicacies you can try!

Balut: A delicacy in the Philippines, Balut is half-hatched chicken eggs (the eggs with legs!).

Kopi Luwak: These are partially-digested coffee beans collected from the poop of the civet, which is a small mammal. Popular in Japan and the US. Don't worry, the beans are washed.

Dormice Stew: A native dish of Slovenia in Europe, the name pretty much says it all. The mice are bred and fattened for cooking.

Fufu: Is an African dish made of mashed yams or plantains and spicy peanut paste.

Sanguinaccio: An Italian pudding made from pig's blood.

P'tcha: A traditional European Jewish jelly made out of calves' hooves.

What's the most exotic dish you've ever eaten?

Ask your friends and family, and document your answers here!

_____

_____

_____

_____

_____

_____

_____

_____

_____

_____

Only the Nose Knows

These noses need faces.

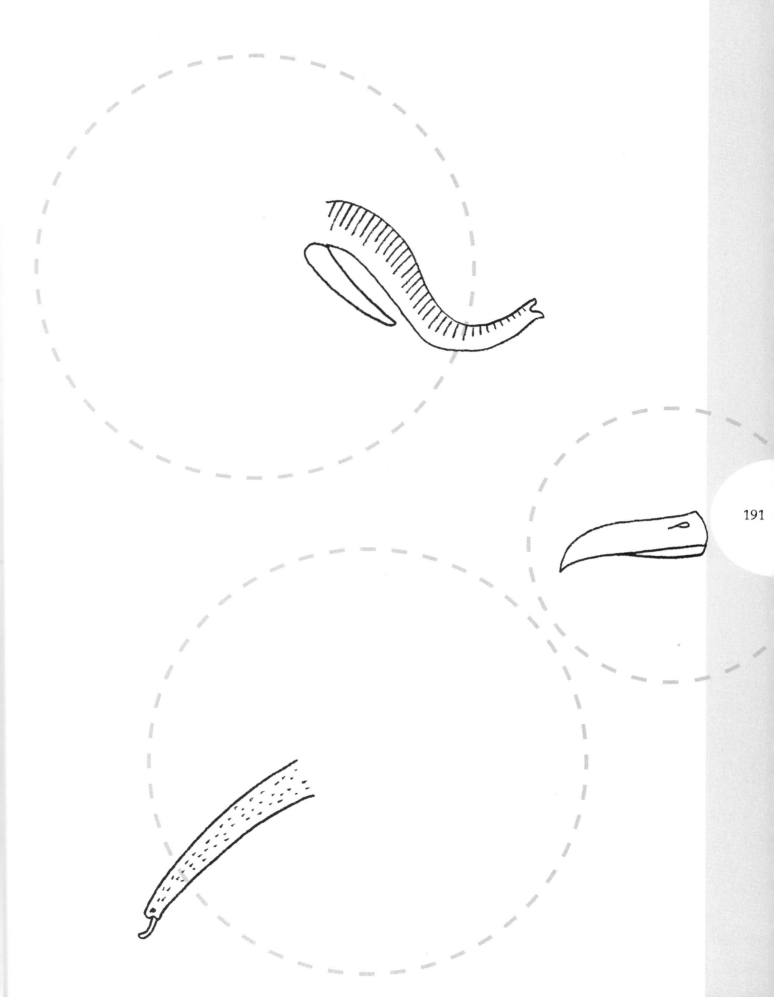

When Nature Calls . . .

. . . you have to listen, right? When traveling abroad, you may find yourself in some stinky situations. To ensure that you find the right place to do your duty, study the names and information below to get where you need to go. Remember to wash your hands!

England & Scotland: W.C. (water closet), Privy, Loo, Bog

Philippines: C.R. (comfort room)

Australia: Dunny or Thunder Bucket (this is for outhouses mostly)

Western Europe: Ask for the Toilet, not the restroom—you don't need to rest, you need a toilet, right?

Paris, France: Be prepared to pay to use a toilet on public streets. Better dig up some change real quick.

Chile: Aldaco (outhouse)

On a ship or boat: The Head

On a military base: Latrines

The John is an American term for the toilet. Hence the little book you may find near your friend's dad's toilet called: *Jokes for the John*.

In parts of Asia and the Middle East you may encounter squatting toilets.

The key-shaped hole in the floor you might find in India is not a drain—it's the toilet. You get the idea. There are also flushable squatting toilets, which you climb up onto.

In Japan, toilets are an art form. Some feature a sensor that opens the lid when you approach, washes you with soap and water, dries you with warm air when complete (no paper needed), and then flushes automatically and closes the lid.

Design the restroom of your dreams here.

On a Roll

Thank the ancient Romans for running water and flushing toilets. Their idea of toilet paper, however, was a sponge soaked in salt water and tied to a stick! Other forms of toilet paper throughout history have included leaves, moss, clay, seashells, corncobs, Sears catalog pages, newspapers, and finally, soft paper on a roll.

Finish These Patterns

Fill these pages with a paisley pattern. The droplet-shaped motif is of Persian and Indian origin. It looks like a very fancy half of the yin-yang symbol. The pattern is sometimes called "Persian pickles" by American quilt makers.

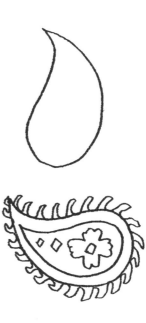

What Are These People Afraid Of?

Monsters, spiders, huge mice, mutant veggies, your teacher?

The Matching Game

This is a game for two players. The object is to connect the duplicate numbers by drawing a line from one to the other.

However, you're not allowed to touch or cross another line. So, player one connects the pair of ones, player two connects the pair of twos, and so on. It's easy at first, but it gets harder as more and more lines are added to page. The last person who can draw a line from one duplicate to another without crossing a line, wins. You can play this game again with blank paper. Simply write pairs of numbers randomly on the page.

198

Welcome to My Beautiful Recreational Vehicle!

RVs aren't just for retired folks. Traveling in an RV means all the comforts of home are at your fingertips. Customize your own by drawing in the features you'd enjoy. What does RECREATION means to you? A balcony, a trampoline, a gigantic popcorn popper, a private screening room? Draw it in.

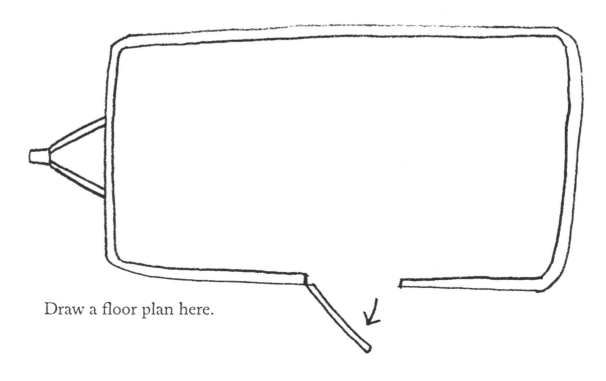

Draw a floor plan here.

Designer Plates

Used to be that license plates had two simple jobs: provide the state the car is registered in and give the car a unique number. Now, most US states allow you to purchase license plates that celebrate a good cause, promote an organization, or even highlights your favorite sports team. The plates are often flashy and fun to look at.

If you're traveling the US this vacation, draw designer plates for the states you visit based on your experiences in that state. So, if you're visiting the coast of North Carolina, and you happen to visit a pirate museum, your plate could look like this:

Then, provide your own letter/number combo to complete the plate. You can create phrases using both letters and numbers such as: "I h8 skool." Most license plates give you eight spaces to create your message.

Car Collecting

Keep track of how many of each type of vehicle you see while on the road. Car dealerships don't count!

Ford Mustang

....

Vehicle with five or more bumper stickers

....

School bus

....

Pick-up truck with something in the truck bed

....

Vehicle with three or more bikes attached to it

....

Any sort of hybrid

....

Volkswagen Beetle (old)

....

Volkswagen Beetle (new)

....

Hummer

....

Cadillac Escalade

....

Corvette

....

Any type of convertible

....

Mini Cooper

....

Police vehicle

....

Car with missing parts

....

Jeep

....

Honda Civic

....

Antique car (at least 25 years old)

....

Fire engine with lights on

....

Add your own favorite vehicles to the mix:

. . . .

List cars/trucks you see that are named after animals:

. . . .

List vehicles named after something in space:

. . . .

List vehicles named after places:

. . . .

What the car company names mean:

VOLKSWAGEN: German for "people's car."

VOLVO: From the Latin word *Volvo*, which means, "I roll."

HONDA: Named after its founder, Soichiro Honda.

HYUNDAI: Means "modern" in Korean.

KIA: Translates as "Rising from Asia."

SUBARU: From the Japanese name for the constellation known as Pleiades or the Seven Sisters.

ISUZU: Named after a river. Means "fifty bells ringing together in celebration."

TOYOTA: Named after the company's founding family.

What's Your Cargo?

Expecting a big shipment? What's being transported here? Draw in the merchandise. Is it coffee beans, furniture, or teddy bears? It's completely up to you.

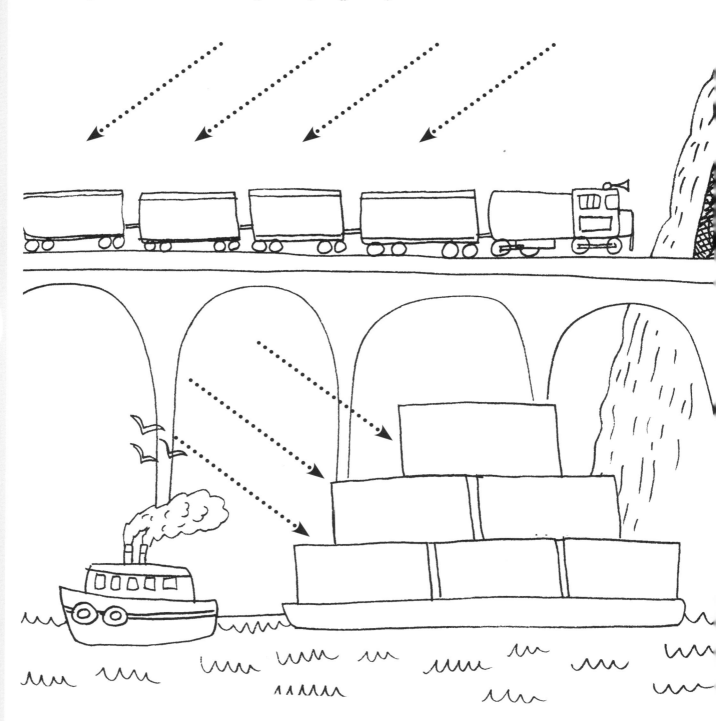

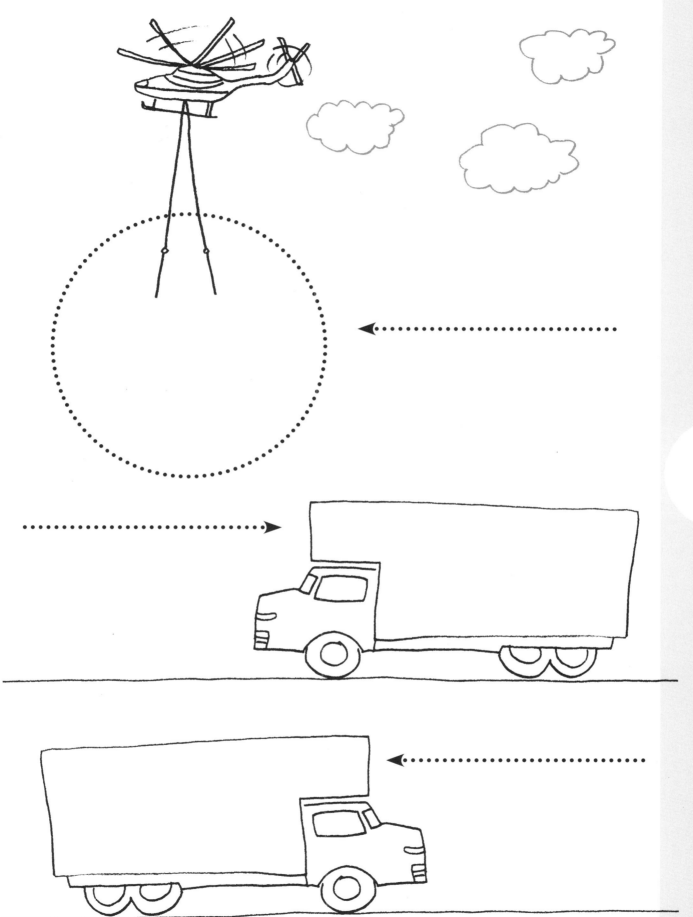

Not Quite There Yet . . .

. . . but very close. Hold it together with these activities.

1 See how long you and one other person can rapidly speak to the other without stopping. It's not as easy as it sounds. WARNING: People sitting near you may not enjoy listening.

2 Find a photo in a book, magazine, or newspaper, and have one of your travel mates attempt to draw the photo using only the descriptions provided by you. Don't tell him/her what it is, just describe it as carefully as possible.

DRAW HERE

abcdefghijklmnopqrstuvwxyz

3 Take turns writing a sentence where each word begins with a consecutive letter of the alphabet.

All Bees Carrying Dreary Elephant Fingernails Get Healing . . .

4 Guess the amount of time it will take until you . . . cross a bridge, see the next billboard, see a herd of cows, stop, get caught in traffic (come up with your own!). Keep a running list of everyone's guesses, and award points for those whose times are closest.

5 Everyone except the driver can play this game. Choose an object out the front window that's far away. All players then close their eyes. When you think the object or place is near, yell, "Now!" The player who opens his/her eyes closest to the object, wins. The driver is the judge.

6 We like to call this game Verb Replacement Therapy. The chooser picks an action verb such as run, jump, cry, or eat, but doesn't tell the other players what it is. The other players then ask questions substituting the phrase "boysenberry" for the verb. For example, say the chooser picked "scratch." A player could ask, "Does a cat boysenberry?" The chooser answers, "Yes, a cat does boysenberry." Sooner or later, someone will figure out the verb.

7 One person selects a category of people, places, or things. The categories could be colors, teachers at school, actors, breakfast foods, etc. Players then take turns listing items in the chosen category. The last player with an answer gets to pick the next category.

Draw the Tree

A tree is holding up all these creatures. What kind is it? It's up to you. Think about whether it's winter, spring, summer, or fall when you're drawing.

Which Came First?

Circle your best guess and ask others what they think.
Then read the answers below!

1. Glue   or   Tape

2. Automobile   or   Bicycle

3. Snaps   or   Zipper

4. Telephone   or   Fax machine

5. Jigsaw Puzzle   or   Yo-Yo

6. Facebook   or   YouTube

7. Hot Dogs   or   Hamburgers

8. Ferris Wheel   or   Roller Coaster

9. Frisbee   or   Hula Hoop

10. Toilet Paper   or   Flushing Toilet

Answers

1 The first glue was patented in Britain around 1750. It was made from fish. Tape was invented in 1925 by Richard Drew, a 3M engineer.

2 The first self-propelled road vehicle was a military tractor invented by a French engineer named Nicolas Joseph Cugnot in 1769. (The first gas-powered cars were developed in the mid to late 1800s, and Henry Ford was the first to make cars readily available in the 1900s.) The invention of the bicycle is attributed to a Scottish blacksmith named Kirkpatrick Macmillan in 1839.

3 Snap fasteners were patented by a German inventor named Heribert Bauer in 1885. The snaps were used for men's pants. Meanwhile, the zipper didn't come along until 1891. It was invented by Witcomb L. Judson, but was greatly improved a few years later in Canada by a Swedish-born electrical engineer.

4 Even though fax machines didn't become common office equipment until the 1980s, the first facsimile machine was invented in 1843 by an Englishman named Alexander Bain. He devise was made up of two pens connected to pendulums, which

in turn were joined to a wire and could reproduce writing on an electrically conductive surface. The telephone, on the other hand, was patented by Alexander Graham Bell in 1876. In fact, another inventor, Elisha Gray, an American inventor who also developed an early fax machine, came up with a device that could also transmit sound electrically. Unfortunately for Gray, Bell reached the patent office just hours before Gray did. There was a fierce legal battle, which Bell won.

5 Yo-yos have been around for more than 2,500 years. In fact, it's considered the second-oldest toy in history. Can you guess what was the first? The doll. Anyway, ancient Greek children played with the toy and decorated the two halves with pictures of gods. The jigsaw puzzle was invented by an English mapmaker and engraver named John Spilsbury in 1767. And what was the first puzzle? A map of the world, of course! Spilsbury's puzzles were used to teach geography to children.

6 The social networking website Facebook was launched in February 2004, while YouTube, the video sharing website, was launched a year later in February 2005.

7 There are lots of claims as to who invented what and when and where, but to the best of our knowledge, hamburgers were first invented around the 1880s-1890s while hot dogs didn't come around until 10-20 years later. The term *hot dog* may have come from a cartoonist who was making fun of the cheap sausage-type food being sold at Coney Island, New York—saying they were made of dog meat. According to one legend, the hamburger originated in Hamburg, New York when two vendors at a county fair ran out of sausages and cooked up some ground-beef patties instead.

8 The first roller coasters were built in France in the early 1800s. The first Ferris Wheel was built for the 1893 World's Fair in Chicago. George W. Ferris, a bridge builder, designed the Wheel to rival the Eiffel Tower.

9 Ancient Egyptian children played with hoops made of vines and dried-out grasses thousands of years ago. The first Frisbee went on sale in 1964, although many colleges claim they had been using Frisbie Baking Company pie tins to play catch with since the 1880s.

10 Toilet paper was first produced for the Emperor of China in 391 AD. Packaged toilet paper for the rest of the world didn't roll around until 1857. And, no, the toilet was not invented by Thomas Crapper. There is evidence of simple toilets dating back 2,800 years; however, Sir John Harrington is credited with inventing a flush toilet in 1596 for Queen Elizabeth I. The first patent for the flushing toilet was given to Alexander Cummings in 1775.

Doodle Their Duds

These tourists packed such plain clothing. Jazz them up with some original doodle patterns! Do something nice, fashionably speaking.

Say Thanks!

Miss Manners will approve! Think of all the people who help and serve you, especially when you're traveling. Leave them a note of thanks for their services or kindness.

Perhaps you'd like to thank the following people:

The waitress who cleaned up the huge mess your baby sister left behind

The porter who carried your gigantic, overstuffed luggage

The cleaning staff at the hotel

The taxi driver who got you there on time

The pilot who landed the plane in a thunderstorm

The mechanic who worked on Saturday to change the broken radiator hose

The flight attendant who cleaned up your barf bag

The ship captain who blew the horn for you

The nice lady who helped you find your parents when they lost you

The kid that was nice to you all week at the resort

Your cousin for sharing her toys and bedroom with you

Your grandparents for giving you spending money for your trip

The chef who made your favorite meal even though it wasn't on the menu

Your parents for taking you on an adventure

See page 221 for tips on writing thank you notes.

Cut out this card and fold it in half. Write your message on the inside and be sure to sign it.

fold here

Thank You!

This is the front of the card. Decorate it with whatever designs or drawings you feel would be appropriate.

This is the inside of the card. Cut it out before you start writing and be sure to do a rough draft before you do your final writing. You can also draw on the inside.

fold here

✂

fold here

THANK YOU!

fold here

Before you write, try a rough draft.

Below is a sample of a thank-you note to use as reference. It's just a suggestion. Please use your own words and artwork for a truly heartfelt thanks. Leave your note where the person can easily find it. It can be short and sweet, and don't forget to sign it.

TODAY'S DATE _____

Dear *Marjory, waitress at Winkies Restaurant*,

Thank you for being so nice to me and my family when you waited on us today at lunch. I realize my grandmother is very particular, and you were so patient with her while she told you how she wanted her sandwich to be prepared. You were also very gracious when she sent it back and ordered something else.

The food was delicious, no matter what Grandma said, and your service was extraordinary.

Sincerely,

_____

YOUR NAME HERE

USE THE SPACE BELOW
for your own rough draft.

WELCOME TO
Café Curlicue

Add fanciful swirls, whorls, and curlicues
to this fashionable sidewalk café.

Menu

Fill in the menu with
foods that have curls
and whorls too.

The World's Famous Places Get a Face-lift . . . From You!

Yellowstone Park's Old Faithful

Sphinx

225

Animal Emblems from Around the World

Animals are often used as a symbol to represent a country. The characteristics of the animal are supposed to reflect the strength of that nation. Kind of like a mascot for a sports team.

The United States uses the symbol of an eagle—you'll find it on American money, flags, and seals. (Some people thought the emblem was so poorly drawn that it looked more like a turkey.) Five other countries also use an eagle as their national animal: Albania, Germany, Nigeria, Mexico, and Poland.

What would your family animal be?

Since you're not a nation, come up with an animal emblem for your family. Answer the questions below and think about which animal reflects the characteristics you feel represent your family, and then draw your family animal on the flag below.

Do you want to show strength, stealth, intelligence, athleticism, wit, goofiness, shyness, hard work, tallness, shortness? What is your family known for?

Match the nation with the animal.

Answers on page 254.

1. Estonia	Beaver
2. France	Bull
3. Iceland	Bear
4. Belarus	Wisent (bison)
5. Bhutan	Water Buffalo
6. Botswana	Pheasant
7. Cambodia	Wolf
8. Vietnam	Kouprey (ox)
9. Nepal	Stag (deer)
10. South Africa	Zebra
11. Ireland	Kiwi
12. Canada	Springbok (gazelle)
13. Honduras	Elephant
14. Italy	Vicuña Llama
15. Thailand	Barn Swallow
16. Japan	White-tailed Deer
17. New Zealand	Condor
18. Chile	Gallic Rooster
19. Peru	Falcon
20. Spain	Takin (antelope)
21. Russia	Cow

227

Make a Mosaic

Mosaic is the art of creating images by assembling small pieces of colored glass, stone, or tiles. Many cultures have used this art to decorate their homes, temples, and marketplaces. Some mosaics are very detailed, while others are simple designs.

Use the square shapes provided here, and on the next spread to make a mosaic design of your own. Fill in squares with a pen or colored pencil. Another way to make a paper mosaic is to cut colored paper and then glue the pieces down to create a design. You can use the blank pages in the back of the book to cut up and create a design, if you wish.

Make a Mosaic

The End?

Like any journey, at some point, you come to the end. But just because we're out of room here, doesn't mean your fun can't continue! We've left a bunch of pages at the back of this book blank for you to do with as you see fit.

Things to Do with Your Blank Pages

* Draw

* Keep a journal

* Create new game boards for the games in this book or continue your favorite activities

* Play hangman or other games we didn't have room for

* Make paper airplanes

* Write a novel

* Write us a note with travel ideas of your own

It's up to you!

Enjoy your travels, no matter where you end up, and we hope to see you again soon!

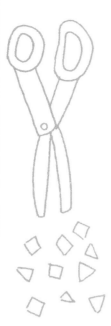

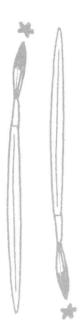

Answer Key

Hinky Pinky
Page 10

1. Large Feline: Fat Cat

2. Small Violin: Little Fiddle

3. Comedian Horse: Silly Filly

4. Tinkerbell needs a shave: Hairy Fairy

5. Lives in the basement: Cellar Dweller

6. Flying horse with no legs: Legless Pegasus

7. A library thief: Book Crook

8. Magical Gecko: Lizard Wizard

9. A sneaky bug: Sly Fly

10. What baby cats wear on their paws:

Kittens' Mittens

11. A hip ghost: Cool Ghoul

12. Rabbit with a sense of humor: Funny Bunny

13. A cool flick: Groovy Movie

14. Sleeping noises that don't excite you:

Boring Snoring

15. Used to fix your sole: Shoe Glue

16. Used to weigh very heavy animals: Whale Scale

17. What you say when a bovine steps on your foot:

"Ow, Cow!"

18. A place for Theodore to sleep: Ted Bed

19. Marching people acting out things without

talking: Charade Parade

20. Burnt money: Cash Ash

21. The White House: President's Residence

Two Truths & a Lie
Page 14

We are not married to each other.

248

Travel Back in Time with
THE SLANG GAME   Page 18

Section 1

DECADE: 1980s

1. Take a chill pill: Relax

2. Tubular: Awesome

3. Gag me with a spoon: Disgusting

4. Gnarly: Beyond extreme

5. Hoser: Loser

6. Have a cow: Get overly excited

7. Rad: Radical

8. Stoked: I am really hopeful

9. Make my day: Don't mess with me

10. Like totally: I agree

Section 2

DECADE:1920s

1. The bee's knees: The best

2. Hard-boiled: Tough

3. Spiffy: Elegant in appearance

4. And how!: I strongly agree

5. Horsefeathers: That's nonsense

6. The big cheese: The boss

7. Flapper: an unconventional

young woman

8. A pill: An unlikeable person

9. Heebie-jeebies: The jitters

10. Putting on the Ritz: Doing

something in a grand manner

Section 3

DECADE: 1960s

1. A gas: A lot of fun

2. Flower child: Hippie

3. Gimme some skin!: Shake my hand

4. Heavy: Deep or cool

5. Ape: Getting crazy angry over something

6. Cool it: Stop

7. Flake off: Go away

8. Groovy: Something great

9. Hang it on me again: Please say that again

10. Bummed out: Depressed

Airport Maze

Page 24

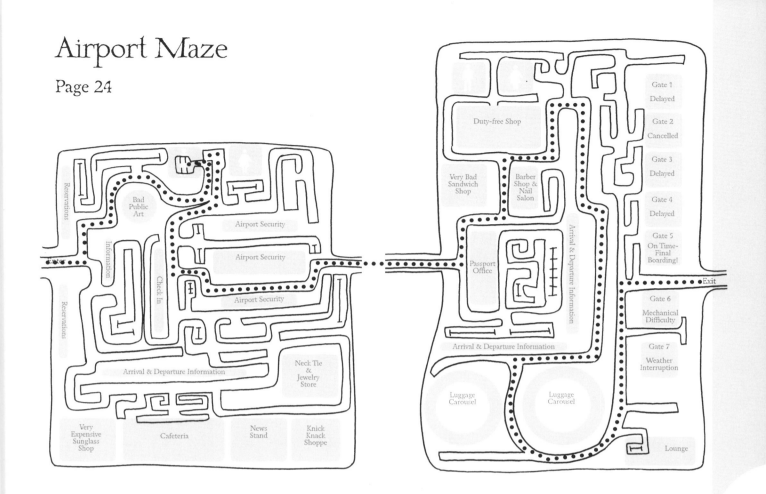

I'm My Own Grandfather

Page 40

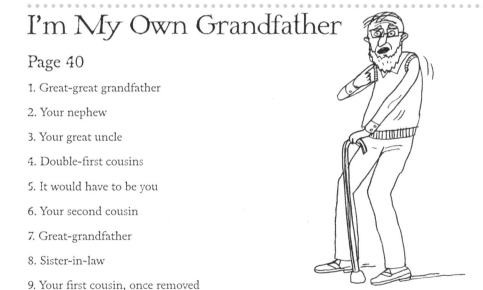

1. Great-great grandfather

2. Your nephew

3. Your great uncle

4. Double-first cousins

5. It would have to be you

6. Your second cousin

7. Great-grandfather

8. Sister-in-law

9. Your first cousin, once removed

10. First, it helps greatly if you're a guy. If not, switch genders. According to the song "I'm My Own Grandpa" by Dwight Latham and Moe Jaffe, first you must marry an older woman with a grown daughter. That daughter is now your stepdaughter. Then, get your dad to marry this daughter. (Don't tell your mom.) Now, this daughter is both your stepdaughter and your stepmother. Your dad is now also your stepson-in-law. Your wife is mother of your stepmother and also your step-grandmother. So, that would make you your own step-grandfather. Did you follow?

IQ Quiz

Page 44

1. None. Roosters don't lay eggs.

2. Moses didn't have an ark. Noah did.

3. Nothing. Buildings can't jump.

4. They weigh the same: 1 pound.

5. There's no dirt in a hole.

6. Seven.

7. Zero

8. All of them.

9. The boat rises with the tide, so if water does cover up three rungs, you're sinking!

10. The match

11. They could be sisters

12. "Incorrectly"

13. e-g-g-w-h-i-t-e

14. Because there's one more penny

15. Half way. After that, you're walking out of the woods.

16. You don't want to bury the survivors now, do you!?

17. Because he's still alive.

18. Henry

19. "Tree" should be "Three"; there should be an "s" at the end of "mistake"; and the third mistake is that there are only two mistakes in this sentence.

20. Give the fifth person the apple in the basket.

21. Three

22. There are no stairs. It's a one-story house.

23. You did.

24. One's a quarter, and the OTHER is a nickel.

25. Electric trains generate no smoke.

Scoring Key

0-25: Don't blame yourself, your brain went on vacation

30-50: Not bad for a beginner

55-100: You're about 2 inches short of genius

105-125: You're a genius . . . or a careful reader

130-200: You took the wrong quiz

Fairy Tales in the News

Page 60

Ball Ends in Chaos as Beautiful Stranger Flees: Cinderella

Giant Carnivore Terrorizes Family: Little Red Riding Hood

Toy Maker Claims Puppet as Son: Pinocchio

Lost Princess Finds True Love . . . : The Princess & the Pea

Siblings Escape Cannibal!: Hansel & Gretel

Daring Prince Kisses 100-year-old Princess: Sleeping Beauty

Girl Charged with Breaking & Entering:

Goldilocks & the 3 Bears

Woman Claims Baked Goods Ran Away:

The Gingerbread Man

Boy Trades Cow for Paltry Sum: Jack & the Beanstalk

Long-Haired Woman Seeks Rescue from Tower: Rapunzel

Trucker Lingo

Page 70

1. The slow lane

2. Blown tire in road

3. 55 miles per hour

4. Unmarked police car

5. Highway

6. A toll booth

7. No police ahead

8. Traffic ticket

9. A rest stop

10. Okay

11. Drive faster

12. A police officer

13. A deer crossing

14. Truck carrying cars or heavy traffic

15. Slow down

16. CB nickname

17. A truck is overweight

18. A small car

19. The trucker you're talking to

20. A car following you too closely

Spot the Tourists

Page 72

. . . .

Find the Hidden Animals

Page 92

1. Scaredy-cat
2. Copycat
3. Cadillac
4. Catastrophe
5. Catalog
6. Cattle
7. Catapult
8. Catacomb
9. Cat scan
10. Caddy
11. Doggy bag
12. Dog tags
13. Hot dog
14. Couch
15. Accountant
16. Coward
17. Kayak
18. Maniac
19. Insomniac
20. Pig tails
21. Piggyback ride
22. Pig Latin
23. Baby
24. Maybe
25. Frisbee

A Different Sort of Alphabet

Page 98

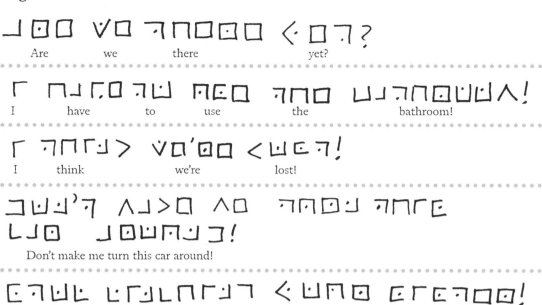

⌐⊟⊟ ∨⊟ ⌐⊓⊟⊟⊟ ＜·⊟⌐?
Are   we   there   yet?

⌐ ⊓⌐⌐⊟⌐⊔ ⊟⊟⊟ ⌐⊓⊟ ⊔⌐⌐⊓⊟⊔⊔⋀!
I   have   to   use   the   bathroom!

⌐ ⌐⊓⊓⌐⌐＞ ∨⊟'⊟⊟ ＜⊔⊟⌐!
I   think   we're   lost!

⌐⊔⌐'⌐ ⋀⌐＞⊟ ∧⊟ ⌐⌐⊟⌐ ⌐⊓⌐⌐ ⌐⌐⊟ ⌐⊟⊔⊓⌐⌐⊏!
Don't make me turn this car around!

⊟⌐⊔⊔ ⊔⌐⌐⊔⊓⌐⌐⌐ ＜⊔⊓⊟ ⊟⌐⌐⌐⊓⊟⊟!
Stop   pinching   your   sister!

Crimez Aginst Grammer

Page 104

The Ultimate Camping & Outdoor Adventure Quiz

Page 118

1. FALSE. As with any physical activity, it's important to stay hydrated. On average, you should have around three quarts of water with you for an easy to moderate hike. If you're going to be climbing to higher altitudes, if there isn't a lot of shade, and if it's hot out, bring more.

2. FALSE. Although there are edible mushrooms to be found along a trail, there are also many poisonous ones, too. It takes an expert to know the difference, and sometimes even they get it wrong.

3. TRUE. Animals, especially bears, will raid your campsite or even your car if they smell food. Find a tree at least 300 feet from your campsite. Use a long rope to suspend your leftovers (in a waterproof bag) from a tree branch. Make sure the bag is 10 feet from the trunk and at least 10 feet off the ground. Put your toothpaste in there, too. (Brush your teeth first!)

4. TRUE. This is for the water's survival, not necessarily yours.

5. FALSE. They may be cute, but they are not cuddly. When it comes to any wild animal, it's best to watch them from a distance and leave them alone.

6. FALSE. No, you can't outrun a bear. They can reach speeds up to 30 mph, and your best defense when encountering a bear is to remain calm, avoid direct eye contact, and slowly walk away without turning your back to him while speaking to him softly. Talk to a park ranger about bear encounters in the area before going on a hike. He or she may have good suggestions for the bears in that particular area. Also remember that bears are not ferocious people eaters. If given the chance, most bears avoid people. Making a lot of noise while hiking, even attaching bells to your pack is one good way to avoid bears to begin with.

7. FALSE. You wouldn't want someone hiking through your backyard, would you? If someone posts a "No Trespassing" sign, they mean it.

8. TRUE. A fire isn't considered "out" until you've followed all of these steps. Make sure you are even allowed to start a campfire before doing so.

9. FALSE. If you keep walking, you'll waste energy and you'll make it even harder for anyone to find you. Carry a whistle with you to make finding you easier.

10. FALSE. This is a sure-fire way of getting lost.

11. TRUE. If you and a buddy get lost, don't separate.

12. TRUE. You can leave a copy of trail you're taking at your campsite or let someone back at home where you're going. And always hike with an adult.

13. TRUE. See #10.

14. FALSE. Tents and fire are not a good combination.

15. FALSE. No matter how clean the water looks, it may contain bacteria that can make you sick. Bring lots of water with you or purchase a water purifying system before camping.

16. FALSE. See # 4.

17. TRUE. This is a little rhyme that will help you stay away from poison ivy and poison oak, which will cause you some pretty uncomfortable itching. If you see three leaves together on the same stem, leave them alone. There are a few very good poison ivy "soap" on the market these days. Pack some before your next outdoor adventure.

18. FALSE. These are not safe hiding places. Your best bet is to squat down low without lying down so that you're not the highest object around. Stand on your pack if you have one. Your best survival technique is to keep tabs on the weather while you're out adventuring. If you feel a sudden drop in temperature and the wind gets stronger, a thunderstorm may be on its way.

19. FALSE. Unless this dude is your uncle Fred, steer clear of outdoor hermit types.

20 FALSE. Give yourself at least a week of slowly breaking in your new hiking boots, wear them for a short time each day.

Animal Emblems
from Around the World

Page 226

1. Estonia: Barn Swallow

2. France: Gallic Rooster

3. Iceland: Falcon

4. Belarus: Wisent (bison)

5. Bhutan: Takin (antelope)

6. Botswana: Zebra

7. Cambodia: Kouprey (ox)

8. Vietnam: Water Buffalo

9. Nepal: Cow

10. South Africa: Springbok (gazelle)

11. Ireland: Stag (deer)

12. Canada: Beaver

13. Honduras: White-tailed Deer

14. Italy: Wolf

15. Thailand: Elephant

16. Japan: Pheasant

17. New Zealand: Kiwi

18. Chile: Condor

19. Peru: Vicuña llama

20. Spain: Bull

21. Russia: Bear